Gaining on the Gap

Changing Hearts, Minds, and Practice

Robert G. Smith, Alvin L. Crawley, Cheryl Robinson, Timothy Cotman Jr., Marty Swaim, and Palma Strand

Published in Partnership with the American Association of School Administrators

ROWMAN & LITTLEFIELD EDUCATION
A division of
ROWMAN & LITTLEFIELD PUBLISHERS, INC.
Lanham • New York • Toronto • Plymouth, UK

Published in partnership with the American Association of School Administrators

Published by Rowman & Littlefield Education
A division of Rowman & Littlefield Publishers, Inc.
A wholly owned subsidary of The Rowman & Littlefield Publishing Group, Inc.
4501 Forbes Boulevard, Suite 200, Lanham, Maryland 20706
www.rowmaneducation.com

Estover Road, Plymouth PL6 7PY, United Kingdom

British Library Cataloguing in Publication Information Available

Library of Congress Cataloging-in-Publication Data

Gaining on the gap : changing hearts, minds, and practice / Robert G. Smith . . . [et al.].
      p. cm.
  "Published in Partnership with the American Association of School Administrators."
  ISBN 978-1-61048-288-2 (cloth : alk. paper)—ISBN 978-1-61048-289-9 (pbk. : alk. paper)—ISBN 978-1-61048-290-5 (electronic)
  1. African Americans—Education—United States—Case studies. 2. Discrimination in education—United States—Case studies. 3. Educational equalization—United States—Case studies. 4. Academic achievement—Social aspects—United States—Case studies. I. Smith, Robert G., 1943– II. American Association of School Administrators.
  LC2717.G35 2011
  371.829'96073—dc22   2011016315

Contents

Foreword

Jay Mathews

In the summer of 1997 I was more full of myself than usual, having just finished the manuscript of my second book about high schools and started a job as an education reporter for the *Washington Post* in the Virginia suburbs. I was already a veteran *Post* reporter, with 26 years at the paper. I had been chief of our bureaus in Hong Kong, Beijing, and Los Angeles, and our Wall Street reporter in New York. I had fallen in love with education reporting. I decided that would be my focus for the rest of my career. I thought I was better at it than anybody.

In that same summer of 1997, it was announced that someone I had never heard of, named Robert G. Smith, had been appointed school superintendent in Arlington County, part of my new beat. Smith had spent several years in one of the Houston area school districts, but this was his first superintendency. He seemed a quiet and modest fellow when I met him, but he began to do things I considered, from my perch as the well-known education author and *Washington Post* reporter, quite outrageous.

When he was being interviewed for the Arlington job, school board member Libby Garvey had asked him why he wanted to come to Arlington. "He said," Garvey told me later, "that many people in education around the nation thought that you could usually predict how a child would do in school if you knew that child's racial and ethnic background. He said he wanted to come to Arlington to prove them wrong."

From the perspective of people who think the best school systems are those with the most affluent students, Arlington was on a downward slide. Less than half of its students by then were non-Hispanic Whites. A third of them were from families poor enough to qualify for federal lunch subsidies.

Many school districts used a growing number of disadvantaged and minority students as an excuse for poor academic performance. Rob Smith did the opposite. He became one of the first district leaders in the country to make closing the achievement gap between Whites and minority students a public goal.

If I had not seen his announcement of his gap-closing plan written down for all to see in a district press release, I would not have believed it. He said he was going to report the level of achievement of all ethnic groups in the county schools every year, and publicly announce whether his schools were closing those gaps or not.

I wrote in the paper that this was a big risk. Reducing ethnic achievement differences would be hard. If the numbers didn't go his way, I would be the first to say so in the major newspaper in his region. The *Post* was closely read every day by a heavy concentration of Arlington voters who, according to some studies, were among the best-read and most politically engaged people in the country.

Smith would look bad. The emphasis on poor minority children might even become a sore point with affluent White parents who worried that their kids would be ignored. Smith's school board, fearful of the next election, had the power to fire him if this went too far. But the more I saw Smith in action, the more I realized that he was not the sort of person who let such fears stand in his way. By the time he retired in 2009, it was clear that he had been right and arrogant doubters like me had been wrong. From 1998 to 2009 the percentage of Arlington students passing the state tests rose from 65% to 90%. Black students went from 37% to 77% and Hispanic students from 47% to 84%. The other ethnic groups improved also, Whites from 82% to 96% and Asians from 69% to 94%. The achievement gaps Smith had resolved to reduce had in fact been reduced. The distance between non-Hispanic White and Black passing rates dropped from 45 to 19 percentage points. Between Hispanics and non-Hispanic Whites, the gap shrank from 35 to 12 percentage points.

At the same time, the county's participation in and success on college-level Advanced Placement, and International Baccalaureate exams climbed, both for affluent and for disadvantaged students. Smith was spreading his message to the rest of the country, co-founding the Minority Student Achievement Network, a group of districts across the country that share information on how to close achievement gaps.

This book is the inside story, by Smith and many of his associates in Arlington, of how they managed to make such progress when skeptics like me doubted it could be done. The writers of the various chapters, including Smith, are among the most talented educators I have known.

You shouldn't take my word for it, of course. You can't trust journalists to keep a firm grip on reality. Smith and his team will tell you what they did and what the results were. Educators this busy rarely have a chance to write down their secrets with such care, so take a look and see how much I missed by underestimating Rob Smith.

Preface

Robert G. Smith

This book came to be as the result of the initiative of a retired teacher and a community member. Marty Swaim and Palma Strand had participated in professional development within the Arlington, Virginia, public school system and in community development directed toward advancing cultural competence to eliminate student achievement gaps based on predictors such as race, income, and dominant language. They believed that their critical work toward eliminating achievement gaps—a focus of the school district for more than a decade—harbored an important story, the telling of which would benefit other school districts and communities.

Marty and Palma invited colleagues who also had been involved in the work to contribute their voice and expertise to a case study that would describe the work in Arlington and serve as a model from which readers in other communities and school districts who share similar goals might extract principles and ideas relevant to them and adapt and apply them to their situations.

One of the strengths of this book is that it presents the perspectives and voices of a variety of people who played a variety of roles in the district's mission to eliminate achievement gaps. It is not a research brief or an impersonal story; we did not shy from first-person accounts because we believe they are of great interest and value to readers.

This case study is not intended to be a cookbook of recipes for action. We recognize that procedural or programmatic solutions applied in one school or one community do not necessarily travel well to other schools and communities. We do hope this book provides hope and suggests some general principles and lessons learned that will enrich the work of schools and communities across the country.

Acknowledgments

We wish to thank a host of people who made possible the experiences that led to the completion of this book. First and foremost we are grateful to the students, staff, parents, and larger community of the Arlington Public Schools: they provided the support necessary for the work portrayed in this volume.

We extend special recognition to those principals, administrators, supervisors, teachers, parents, and community members whose work we mention directly, if not by name, in recounting our journey. We acknowledge especially the efforts of the teacher leaders who participated in the various forms of cultural competence training described in these pages and the teachers and administrative staff who led the training. We acknowledge also the important contributions of the principals and supervisors who worked to create the conditions that engaged students in rigorous experiences and the staff who served on the Council for Cultural Competence.

We also applaud the parents and community members who served on one or more of the advisory committees such as the Superintendent's Advisory Committee on the Elimination of the Achievement Gap, the Superintendent's Advisory Committee on Accountability and Evaluation, and the Advisory Council on Instruction.

We extend, as well, our thanks to a succession of outstanding Arlington school board members. Without their support and commitment, the work depicted here would have been impossible. Libby Garvey, the current chair of the board, deserves special recognition as the one member who served during the entire time represented in this book; she has supported the work

Acknowledgments

we describe throughout her service. Frank Wilson, a recently retired school board member of 24 years who dedicated his extraordinary service to the goal of overcoming achievement gaps, also merits special mention.

We recognize also the invaluable perspectives and support provided by the Minority Student Achievement Network.

The rendering of this journey would have been much less clear and accessible in the absence of the assistance and sage advice of Rowman and Littlefield's Vice President for Education Tom Koerner and Assistant Editor Lindsey Schauer and the editing of Pat Carroll.

We recognize and appreciate the contributions of all of these people but accept full responsibility for any inelegant language, mistakes in the description of events, omissions of relevant information, and other faults found in the text.

Introduction

Palma Strand

Closing achievement gaps is a mantra of American education. The passage of the No Child Left Behind legislation (NCLB) in 2001 cemented it as one of the central goals in the national focus on school improvement. School districts across the country must report achievement gaps for a variety of groups and must demonstrate "adequate yearly progress" for each of those groups.

Closing achievement gaps is, in the minds of a number of scholars and leaders, the most important civil rights issue of the 21st century. Eliminating achievement gaps for the purposes of this discussion means removing the power of prediction from certain variables that currently explain student achievement: It does not suggest that all students will reach the same outcomes, but it does mean that the outcomes reached will depend on factors other than race/ethnicity, socioeconomic status, or dominant language.

The Arlington Public Schools (APS) in Arlington County, Virginia, began grappling with issues of education quality and diversity, and with achievement gaps, several years before NCLB. In this volume, we chronicle and reflect on APS's work on these issues over the past dozen years. We make no claim to have discovered a "silver bullet," revealed what works best in all situations, or created a model for others to imitate. Part of what we have concluded, in fact, is that the specific path to be trod by each school and school system is unique because each school and school system is unique.

We do believe, however, that we have made significant progress and that we have learned some lessons worth sharing with colleagues and communities engaged in this work. In particular, we have begun a shift from viewing achievement gaps as resulting from problems with the children who come to our schools to viewing them as resulting from problems with the school systems to which these children come.

This perspective does not deny the relevance of other factors such as poverty; level of parent education; social supports such as medical care, quality child care, and preschool; and per-pupil spending. It does, however, keep school systems "on the hook" as being a significant cause of perpetuating or widening achievement gaps. Because school systems *do* have a significant set of contributing factors within their control, they cannot in good conscience excuse inaction by blaming other factors. They must take responsibility for doing as much as is within their power to eliminate such gaps.

The most glaring set of achievement gaps in APS relate to race and ethnicity: On multiple measures, Black and Latino students do not do as well as White students. An initial step for a school system taking responsibility for these outcomes (rather than pointing an accusing finger at students, their families, or other factors) is to acknowledge that they are a manifestation of institutional racism.

Institutional racism encompasses racial disparities that result from institutional structures and operations, although generally not from overt acts of intentional discrimination (Tatum 1999). Institutional racism is entrenched, intractable, and not easily eradicated, in part because those who perpetuate it are often not even aware that they are doing so and in part because it operates through the cumulative actions of multiple people rather than as a single readily identifiable act of one individual.

Tackling institutional racism thus means taking responsibility and looking for solutions *as a system*. This approach entails first acknowledging the results of the system's actions. To be meaningful, this step must be grounded in concrete and reliable data. Data are essential because they provide benchmarks for measuring progress and thus a basis for system accountability—to all of those involved.

More deeply, because of the accretive nature of the system's "actions," a systemic initiative to narrow or eliminate achievement gaps requires the participation of all those who comprise the system, especially teachers and other instructional personnel. Because institutional racism manifests itself as the cumulative result that emerges from the actions of all individuals in the system, only changes in those individual contributions will change the overall result.

Awareness of the need for system-wide contributions to addressing achievement gaps caused APS to develop an internal cultural competence training for teachers and other instructional personnel that not only addresses diversity but calls for self-reflection as to privilege and the accoutrements of privilege. This training is only one part of the system's larger minority achievement effort, but we highlight it because the need for it became clear only after other initiatives to decrease gaps yielded concrete but flat-lining progress. Changing systems, policies, and protocols went only so far.

Cultural competence training seeks to reach and change the hearts, minds, and practices of the myriad individuals within the system. From these widespread changes, we believe, will emerge change in the character, and thus in the outcomes, of the system as a whole. In this way, the institutional racism that now characterizes the school system—a structural racism that is manifested through the culture of the organization—is challenged directly through the dismantling of the old culture and the creation of a new one.

As those within APS change their behavior in response to cultural competence training, the culture of the system will change. The system's culture has historically perpetuated and accepted achievement gaps in multiple ways. The culture now being nurtured—in classrooms, in hallways and cafeterias, in counseling offices, in interactions with parents—does not tolerate such gaps.

Change must in turn be documented not just in terms of overall system results but in terms of interim steps. While the cultural competence training to change the institutional culture is well underway, the documentation process is just beginning. Our vision is that, over time, best practices will change, confidence that the gaps can be tackled successfully will grow, and the culture of institutional racism that supports achievement gaps will be superseded.

The conversation about race and achievement gaps that has been driving this shift in Arlington has been enriched by the contributions of many different people inside and outside the school system. In fact, the participation of different people in different roles has—at least in Arlington—been essential first to the realization of the systemic nature of achievement gaps and then to the evolution of system-wide initiatives to address them. Initiatives and buy-in have both grown from this conversation.

The six authors of this book represent distinct voices in this conversation. The voices include superintendent, two levels of administrator, teacher, cultural competence trainer, community member, and parent. Specifically, we are

- the former superintendent of schools (Rob Smith)
- a parent and community member who has been involved in training initiatives for community and staff participants (Palma Strand)
- the supervisor of minority achievement in the APS Division of Instruction (Cheryl Robinson)
- a minority achievement coordinator who works with students, parents, and teachers (Tim Cotman)
- a retired teacher who conducts training on issues of race, culture, and school achievement (Marty Swaim)
- the assistant superintendent for student services, who heads a Council on Cultural Competence (Alvin Crawley)

These individual voices relate key events and initiatives from six distinct vantage points. The resulting account of the APS story is neither chronological nor linear, and the stories are not discrete. But these overlapping perspectives, taken together, convey a sense of how systemic change happens through different people acting in their own capacities in their own spheres and changing how they operate. It is when this happens that the institution and the institutional culture begin to shift, which we see as an essential step in eradicating institutional racism.

In Chapter 1, Rob Smith and Palma Strand set the context for the APS initiative to close achievement gaps with some historical background and a description of APS and the Arlington, Virginia, community.

A mere generation ago, Arlington was a Black-and-White segregated school system. Desegregation and then significant immigration—first primarily Asian and then Latino—changed community and school demographics. A continuing pattern of segregated housing, however, has led to schools with markedly different demographics throughout the county even today. Overall, APS is now a White plurality (48%) school system that enjoys strong public support and funding.

In Chapter 2, Rob turns his focus to the organization conditions that are required to close achievement gaps. He suggests that for school systems to succeed in closing achievement gaps they must

- admit that they have a problem and put the data that demonstrate the problem front-and-center in a form that can be easily understood;
- measure and report progress consistently;
- make the goal of eliminating or narrowing gaps a priority for everyone in the organization in a way that is addressed by every school and every teacher and is reflected in system, school, department, administrator, and teacher plans for which they are held accountable; and
- implement interventions that focus on key variables early and consistently.

In Chapter 3, Rob describes some of the issues that have arisen in the APS efforts to systematically address achievement gaps and strategies for addressing those issues. These include the need to build a coalition of support for taking on achievement gaps as a systemic priority, the interaction between this and other system priorities, and how internal friends and external allies have proven invaluable in moving forward.

In Chapter 4, Palma Strand, who served on the Superintendent's Advisory Committee on the Elimination of the Achievement Gap from 2000 to 2006 and who participated in an early stage of the development of the cultural competence training, describes the shift from a student-deficit approach to a system-centered approach.

The systems approach acknowledges institutional racism and counters it directly through cultural competence. Palma's perspective is that of both outsider and insider, which allows her to see both the system as a whole and what happens within it. Her discussion highlights the insights a systems understanding has to offer and the way such an understanding reinforces a cultural competence approach.

In Chapter 5, Supervisor for Minority Achievement Cheryl Robinson describes key factors that led to the development of a system-wide cultural competence initiative and offers her perspective on the events, institutional arrangements, and confluence of circumstances that were particularly significant in moving the training initiative forward.

As the staff liaison to the Superintendent's Advisory Committee, the manager of a pivotal federal GEAR UP grant, and the Department of

Instruction point person on achievement gaps, Cheryl has been in a central position in the school system vis-à-vis its efforts on the issue.

The APS cultural competence training has, we believe, some key characteristics that enhance its effectiveness:

- Although it draws from multiple trainings and sources, it was developed internally, which maximizes its "fit" with APS as well as buy-in from those responsible for administering it.
- It begins with self-reflection, identity, and White privilege, which emphasize that the training is not about changing others' behavior but our own.
- It uses stories—literary, personal, and guest speakers—to build empathy and understanding so that it operates on the "heart" as well as the "head."
- It allows time, to the extent possible, recognizing that transformations in people's views and actions happen incrementally and often slowly.
- It incorporates practical applications in the form of difficult conversations with others and pedagogical strategies so that "change agents" have concrete tools for change.
- It started with a small group of APS employees who volunteered to be trained themselves and then agreed to provide training to others; it has progressed to include a larger and larger segment of APS instructional staff, building on the "early adaptors" as it has grown.

In Chapter 6, Minority Achievement Coordinator Tim Cotman provides a vivid description of how cultural competence training leads to personal "aha!" moments of self-awareness that serve as the foundation for changing individual behavior, particularly in the classroom.

Tim's description is based on two precursors to the current APS cultural competence training model that were offered to APS instructional staff on a voluntary basis: IT MATTERS (Improving Total Minority Achievement Through Teacher Experiential-Related Seminars) and SEED (Seeking Educational Equity and Diversity), both of which provided opportunities for teachers to discuss issues of race and ethnicity in a supportive environment over an extended period.

In Chapter 7, former classroom teacher and current cultural competence trainer Marty Swaim uses concrete examples of teacher research to show how cultural competence training can lead to changes in teaching and different classroom outcomes.

Marty's class Teaching Across Cultures, another precursor to the current cultural competence training, used literature and parent speakers from Black, Latino, and Asian cultures to give teachers a familiarity with the home cultures of their students and the experiences of students and parents of color in APS. Teachers reflected on these materials in personal writing and, as the class progressed, undertook small-scale research projects as part of the class.

In Chapter 8, Assistant Superintendent for Student Services Alvin Crawley describes another important contributor to the systemic changes described here: the Council for Cultural Competence, a committee of APS employees from throughout the system (not limited to instructional personnel) that has served as a key forum in which "diversity" issues and achievement gaps could be meshed into the system-level initiative of cultural competence.

Having a system-wide structure was essential to the decision to undertake a diversity audit in 2003. The council now works with the Department of Instruction in cultural competence training, and Alvin describes in this chapter how cultural competence training is being taken to scale within the system.

Following the separate chapters, each of us offers individual "Lessons Learned" from our own perspective in the work (Rob's appear after Chapter 3). Finally, in Chapter 9, we collectively review what we have learned from the past dozen years and what might be of use to other school systems grappling with similar issues.

We begin Chapter 9 with a summary of the progress made by APS as evidenced by measurable accomplishments related to eliminating achievement gaps. Reflecting on the changes made over the past dozen years, we identify four stages in the evolution of the work. Probing still deeper, we discern a number of shared central ideas regarding achievement gaps that have emerged over time. These include the following:

- The existence of external social factors cannot let school systems "off the hook" with respect to achievement gaps: Whatever is within their purview, they must act on. The still-indeterminate nature of how much schools can accomplish calls them to over- rather than underestimate their ability to make a difference.
- This can't just be the work of "the Black guy on the board," the Black and Latino community, or one superintendent or school board. Part of

the work thus has to be to expand the base in terms of who cares, who will keep pushing the issue, and to build in sustainability over time.

- An awareness of the systemic nature of the problem is important; contributing to this awareness are not only policies such as strategic plan goals but system-wide structures such as the Council on Cultural Competence and the Superintendent's Advisory Committee on the Elimination of the Achievement Gap.
- This work is a long-term proposition; the ripples spread slowly over time, though at an accelerated pace after a certain point.
- As progress is made, new horizons and new imperatives appear; changes in the status quo call for new strategies, adjustments in direction, and innovative ideas for continuing to move forward.

The cultural competence training that is the current "cutting edge" of work on achievement gaps in APS embodies these central ideas.

Chapter 9 continues with a look at three themes that recur throughout the various perspectives we present in this book: (1) "outing" race, or being explicit about race and racial experiences; (2) a shared conviction that this work is necessary; and (3) building in systemic sustainability as a necessary component of eradicating entrenched institutional racism. The chapter concludes with a summary of "Lessons Learned" that pulls together the individual perspectives offered throughout the book.

REFERENCE

Tatum, Beverly D. 1999. *Why Are All the Black Kids Sitting Together in the Cafeteria? And Other Conversations about Race: A Psychologist Explains the Development of Racial Identity*. New York: Basic Books.

Chapter One

The Context

Robert G. Smith and Palma Strand

A SMALL SLICE OF HISTORY

Arlington County sits across the Potomac River from Washington, DC. As was the case in much of the United States in 1954, the Arlington Public Schools (APS) were racially segregated by law. At that time, Black and White were the only significant racial/ethnic groups in Arlington. Three small elementary schools served the three predominantly Black neighborhoods in the county—Halls Hill, later Highview Park, in North Arlington; Green Valley, later Nauck, in South Arlington; and Johnson Hill, later Arlington View, also in South Arlington.

For junior and senior high school, Black students attended Hoffman-Boston, located in Johnson Hill. Even students who lived in the Halls Hill area of North Arlington, within walking distance of all-White Stratford Junior High School and Washington-Lee Senior High School, were bused past those schools to the county's segregated secondary school approximately five miles to the south.

As to its public schools, Arlington was notable vis-à-vis other Virginia jurisdictions in two important respects: (1) school board members were elected rather than appointed; and (2) the Black population was relatively small, on the order of 10% of the whole.

In response to the *Brown v. Board of Education* decision by the Supreme Court in 1954 and *Brown II*, which set the "all deliberate speed" standard a year later, Arlington formulated mild, voluntary integration measures. The state of Virginia, however, adopted the stance and strategy of "massive resistance," which called for the state to suspend

9

any compliance with *Brown* until the Constitution was amended to support it.

Concurrently, an NAACP lawsuit led to a federal court decision in 1956 ordering APS to desegregate. The NAACP chose to litigate in Arlington because:

- The strongly anti-integration Byrd political machine was weak there, as evidenced in part by the local ability to elect school board members—a prerogative that had resulted from local efforts to improve the quality of the public schools in the 1940s.
- Blacks were a small minority, which resulted in desegregation being less threatening to Whites.
- The White population was ambivalent about rather than vehemently opposed to *Brown*, a phenomenon attributed to Arlington's heavy population of federal workers.

Although Arlington was now subject to a federal court order mandating desegregation, it was also bound by the Virginia massive resistance legislation. For the next two-and-a-half years, until massive resistance was declared unconstitutional by the state and federal courts in 1959, the state legislation effectively preempted the federal court order, and the APS desegregation status remained in limbo.

Following the rulings that removed state-erected barriers to the enforcement of *Brown*, four Black students from Halls Hill desegregated previously all-White Stratford Junior High School in February 1959. Stratford was the first school in Virginia to desegregate, and there was significant White support for the enrollment of the Black students, although Black parents continued to take the lead (Gates 1965; Micheloti 1988; Morris 2001; Peltason 1961).

During the next 12 years, desegregation progressed in discrete steps. The all-Black high school at Hoffman-Boston was closed, and then the junior high school. Finally, in 1971, in response to another NAACP lawsuit, all-Black Drew Elementary School in Green Valley was closed as a neighborhood school and its students bused throughout the county. Arlington was declared a "unitary" system (Hart 1971). The first Black school board member was selected by appointment in 1971. (Part of the fallout from the confrontation between Arlington and the state of Virginia over desegregation had been the rescission of the provision for the election of the school board.)

For the next two decades, Arlington's school population dipped and then rose again as a result of demographic trends. Schools closed during the enrollment decline, which left the remaining schools crowded when the population rebounded. Waves of immigrants arrived—first from Southeast Asia and then from Latin America. Beginning around 1970, while the percentage of Arlington's population that was Black remained constant, the White percentage shrank and the Asian and Latino percentages grew. By 2000, 28% of the total population of Arlington was foreign-born.

By the early 1990s, the school system faced significant issues of crowding and diversity. The school board and superintendent called for a comprehensive citizen process—"Futures"—to propose how to address these concerns. From this process emerged a distinct community concern with education equity, the first time the issue had been articulated as such. Around the same time, a civic initiative to reclaim the right to elect the school board came to fruition, and leaders from the Futures process were elected to serve on the school board.

When the time came in 1997 to select a new superintendent, the issues of education quality and equity and their interaction with race and ethnicity had come to the forefront. One of the primary criteria in seeking the new person for the job, then, became his or her awareness of and commitment to addressing these issues. The school board decided Dr. Rob Smith was the candidate who best fit the bill.

ARLINGTON AND THE ARLINGTON PUBLIC SCHOOLS

The school system to which Rob came as superintendent combined a rich history of strong support for public education and a compact geography (Arlington is one of the smallest counties in the United States) with a changed landscape both in terms of a much more diverse population than had historically been the case and an environment that, while retaining significant single-family residential areas, also had urbanized dramatically since the opening of Metrorail in the 1970s.

Arlington's approximately 209,000 residents are about 65% White, 8% Black, 9% Asian, and 16% Latino. In addition to the rich diversity represented in its robust immigrant population, Arlington County boasts a well-educated adult population, with the highest proportion (38%) of graduate degrees among all U.S. counties; a relatively high standard of living with a $99,000, 2008 median income for a family of four; and high property wealth, well balanced between residential and commercial (Arlington County 2009).

In this densely populated county, the approximately 20,000 Arlington Public Schools students are distributed across 35 schools and programs. Not surprisingly given the overall demographics of the county, the student body is quite diverse: 48% White, 13% Black, 11% Asian, and 27% Latino. Three characteristics of the APS demographics are especially noteworthy:

• There is no racial or ethnic group that constitutes a majority of the system.
• The school demographics differ significantly from those of the county's population overall.
• In the APS population, minority groups comprise a greater proportion of the whole than in the general population.

About a third of the students receive free or reduced-price meals, 42% speak a first language other than English, and 28% receive English for Speakers of Other Languages services. Representatives of 128 different nations of origin and speakers of 95 different first languages populate that group. The most frequent first language, other than English, is Spanish (about 70% of second-language students), followed by Amharic, Arabic, Mongolian, and Bengali (about 3% or 4% each).

As with the general population, school staff demographics differ from the student population. More than three-quarters of the teaching faculty have earned a master's degree or higher and about 80% are female. By race and ethnicity among teachers, counselors, librarians, and other instructional non-teaching staff, White educators predominate at 78% of the total, with Black and Latino staff accounting for 11% and 8% respectively. Among administrative staff (i.e., principals, assistant principals, other administrative staff, and some technical staff), White personnel represent 68% of the total.

Latino (5%) and Black (25%) staff account for most of the other administrative staff. Among the remaining personnel (subtracting administrative and teaching/instructional staff), Latino, Black, and White staff each constitute about 30% of the group, followed by Asians at 10%. Across all staff, the White majority represents 57% of the total, followed by Black (19%), Latino (18%), and Asian (6%) personnel. (See Table 1.1 in Appendix.)

COMMUNITY, PARENT, AND
TEACHER PERCEPTIONS AND SUPPORT

Before and during Rob's tenure as superintendent, the Arlington Public Schools benefited from an extraordinarily supportive community, which during the past two decades voted positively on every-other-year school construction bond referenda at a rate exceeding 70%. The community has also provided generous budget support, with its per-pupil expenditures at or near the top of the state. This support has continued unabated as APS grappled with education quality and diversity and, after Rob's arrival, made an explicit commitment to closing achievement gaps (more on this in Chapter 2).

Grading the Public Schools

In the past 10 years, parents and community members more broadly have expressed considerable satisfaction with the schools. For example, when answering the Gallup Poll question about what grade they would give the schools in Arlington, parents have given increasingly positive grades over time. In 1999, 77% of parents gave APS an "A" or "B," with 24% giving an "A." In 2009, 94% gave either an "A" or "B," with 57% giving an "A"—more than double the 1999 percentage of "A"s. (See Table 1.2 in Appendix.)

Similarly, community members (defined as adult residents who do not currently have children attending the Arlington Public Schools) gave increasingly positive marks to the Arlington Public Schools over the years from 2002 (the first year the Arlington Public Schools sampled community members) to 2009, moving from giving 46% "A" or "B" in 2002 to 77% "A" or "B" in 2009 and from 16% "A" in 2002 to 37% "A" in 2009. Nearly as positive in terms of engaging the community at large, the proportion of "don't know" responses fell from 44% in 2002 to 15% in 2009. (See Table 1.3 in Appendix.)

Perceptions about the Achievement Gap

The community also joined parents and teachers in expressing strong support for closing achievement gaps. Nearly three-quarters of Arlington Public School parents and two-thirds of community members in 2007 and 2009 rated closing the gap as "very important." In 2009, 70% of the teachers agreed that closing the achievement gap was important. Among all three groups, there were no statistically different responses by race or ethnicity (Arlington Public Schools 2009). (See Table 1.4 in Appendix.)

In 2009, parents, community members, and teachers were also asked the Gallup Poll question: "Do you believe the achievement gap can be narrowed substantially while maintaining high standards for all children?" This question was asked because many school districts that take on the work of addressing achievement gaps report resistance to the goal if supporters of other initiatives (e.g., proponents of education for the gifted) believe their interests will suffer. (See Table 1.5 in Appendix.)

Although more than three-quarters of Arlington respondents in 2009 supported the proposition that achievement gaps can be narrowed while maintaining high standards for all children (70% of teachers answered "yes" in 2007) (Arlington Public Schools 2009), they are slightly less likely to subscribe to that belief than in the 2006 national sample of parents and community members (Rose and Gallup 2006). Similar to the response on the importance of narrowing achievement gaps, no statistically different responses on agreement with the proposition were recorded for Arlington respondents by race or ethnicity.

As will be discussed in succeeding chapters, scholars, legislators, teachers, administrators, parents, and community members are divided over the degree to which schools can close achievement gaps and whether they should be held accountable for doing so. The Gallup Poll tried to determine public perceptions on that issue by asking the question: "In your opinion, is it the responsibility of the public schools to close the achievement gap between White students and Black and Hispanic students?" (See Table 1.6 in Appendix.)

About two-thirds of Arlington teachers and parents and a clear majority of community members see closing achievement gaps as a responsibility of the Arlington Public Schools. A somewhat surprising proportion of teachers (20% and 22% in 2007 and 2009 respectively) responded "don't know" (Arlington Public Schools 2009). Discussions with teachers who advised the school system on this question, revealed that a reasonable explanation for this response may be that rather than disavowing the school's responsibility for closing achievement gaps, these teachers believed that schools cannot succeed without parents also taking responsibility for student achievement.

In the 2009 Arlington response, White parents were more likely than minority parents to agree that closing achievement gaps is the responsibility of the schools, and Hispanic parents were most likely to disagree with that proposition. Among teachers, elementary and female teachers were more likely than secondary and male teachers respectively to agree with the proposition.

Finally, in the 2009 survey, Arlington respondents were asked to rate how successful their schools have been in narrowing gaps by responding to the question: "In your opinion, how successful do you think Arlington Public Schools has been in narrowing the academic achievement gap between minority and White students?"

The most frequent or modal response for all groups was "somewhat successful," and although more than 80% of teachers and nearly three-fourths of parents believe Arlington Public Schools has been at least somewhat successful, slightly less than half of community members agree, with nearly 30% of them indicating they are unsure. There were no statistically different responses by race or ethnicity; however, older teachers were more likely than younger teachers to believe the schools had been successful (Arlington Public Schools, 2009). (See Table 1.7 in Appendix.)

These poll data, along with the tangible community contributions to the public schools in per-pupil spending and bond approvals, drive home the extraordinary support APS has enjoyed from the Arlington community as a whole. This is particularly significant because over this period the school demographics have diverged from the overall demographics of the county: The student population is significantly more Black, Asian, and Latino and less well off socioeconomically. Moreover, there has been increased focus on both the existence of achievement gaps and on the high priority given to addressing them. Despite these changes, Arlington's commitment to public education remains strong.

APPENDIX

Table 1.1. Number and Percent of School Staff by Race/Ethnicity by Gender: 2008–2009

Type of Staff/ Gender	Race/Ethnicity											
	Asian		Black		Latino		White		Other		Total	
	No.	%	No.	%	No.	%	No.	%	No.	%	No.	%*
Teacher Scale	58	3	205	11	161	8	1504	78	11	1	1939	101
Female	49	3	161	10	130	8	1199	77	11	1	1550	99
Male	9	2	44	11	31	8	305	78	0	0	389	99
Administrative	1	1	32	25	6	5	86	68	1	1	126	100
Female	0	0	23	25	4	4	66	71	0	0	93	100
Male	1	3	9	27	2	6	20	61	1	3	33	100
Classified/Other	163	10	457	29	487	30	483	30	13	—	1603	99
Female	77	7	289	27	356	33	346	32	7	1	1075	100
Male	86	16	168	32	131	25	137	26	6	1	528	100
Total	222	6	694	19	654	18	2073	57	25	1	3668	101
Female	126	5	473	17	490	18	1611	59	18	1	2718	100
Male	96	10	221	23	164	17	462	49	7	1	950	100

*Percent may not total 100 owing to rounding

Table 1.2. Grades Given to Their Community Schools by Arlington Parents by Percent by Year: 1999–2009

Grade	Year				
	1999	2002	2004	2007	2009
A	24	40	46	48	57
B	53	46	46	43	37
C	18	9	7	8	4
D	4	2	2	—	—
F	—	—	—	1	
Don't Know		3	1	1	1

Table 1.3. Percent of Grades Given by Community Members to the Arlington Public Schools: 2002–2009

Grade	Year			
	2002	2004	2007	2009
A	16	13	27	37
B	30	25	42	40
C	9	10	7	7
D	1	1	1	—
F	1	1		1
Don't Know	44	49	23	15
Refused	—	1	1	—

Table 1.4. Percent of Arlington Parents, Community Members, and Teachers Rating the Importance of Closing the Achievement Gap

Rating	Parent		Community Member		Teacher
	2007	2009	2007	2009	2009
Very Important	74	74	67	66	70
Somewhat Important	17	19	23	21	18
Somewhat Unimportant	2	3	3	4	2
Very Unimportant	2	1	3	3	8
Don't Know/Unsure	4	3	4	4	2
Refused	1	—	—	1	—

Table 1.5. Percent of Arlington Parent, Community Member, and Teacher Responses on Whether Achievement Gaps Can Be Narrowed While Maintaining High Standards for All Children: 2007 and 2009

Response	Parent		Community		Teacher	
	2007	2009	2007	2009	2007	2009
Yes	81	79	79	75	70	78
No	12	13	11	15	12	6
Don't Know	6	8	10	11	17	—
Refused	2	—	1	—	—	—

Table 1.6.   Percent of Arlington Parent, Community Member, and Teacher Responses on the Question of Whether Schools Are Responsible for Closing Achievement Gaps: 2007 and 2009

Rating	Parent		Community		Teacher	
	2007	2009	2007	2009	2007	2009
Yes	68	64	68	57	62	69
No	25	29	21	27	18	9
Don't Know	5	6	9	15	20	22
Refused	2	1	1	—	—	—

Table 1.7.   Percent of Arlington Parent, Community Member, and Teacher Responses on the Question of How Successful the Arlington Public Schools Has Been in Narrowing Achievement Gaps

Response	Group		
	Parent N=605	Community N=601	Teacher N=632
Very Successful	19	7	17
Somewhat Successful	55	42	65
Somewhat Unsuccessful	6	8	7
Very Unsuccessful	1	1	2
Don't Know/Unsure	8	29	2
Refused	—	1	—
Need More Information/No Basis to Judge	11	11	7

REFERENCES

Arlington County. 2009. *Profile 2009*. Arlington, VA: Planning Research, Analysis and Graphics Section of the Department of Community Planning, Housing and Development.

Arlington Public Schools. 2009. *2009 Community Satisfaction Survey Results*. Arlington, VA: Author.

Bushaw, William J., and Alec M. Gallup. 2008. "Americans Speak Out—Are Educators and Policy Makers Listening? The 40th Annual Phi Delta Kappa/ Gallup Poll of the Public's Attitudes toward the Public Schools. " *Phi Delta Kappan* 90(1): 9–20.

Gates, Robbins L. 1964. *The Making of Massive Resistance: Virginia's Politics of Public School Desegregation*, 1954–1956. Chapel Hill: University of North Carolina Press.

Hart v. County School Board of Arlington County, Virginia, 329 F. Supp. 953 (E.D. Va. 1971).

Michelotti, Cecelia. 1988. "Arlington School Desegregation: A History." *The Arlington Historical Magazine* 8(4).

Morris, James McGrath. 2001. "A Chink in the Armor: The Black-Led Struggle for School Desegregation in Arlington, Virginia, and the End of Massive Resistance." *Journal of Policy History* 13(3): 329–366.

Peltason, J.W. 1961. *Fifty-eight Lonely Men: Southern Federal Judges and School Desegregation*. New York: Harcourt, Brace & World.

Rose, Lowell C., and Alec M. Gallup. 2006. "The 38th Annual Phi Delta Kappa/Gallup Poll of the Public's Attitudes toward the Public Schools." *Phi Delta Kappan* 88(1): 41–53.

———. 2007. "The 39th Annual Phi Delta Kappa/Gallup Poll of the Public's Attitudes toward the Public Schools." *Phi Delta Kappan* 89(1): 33–48.

Chapter Two

Creating Organization Conditions to Close Achievement Gaps

Robert G. Smith

Our experiences, along with observed experiences of other school districts, suggest that for school systems to succeed in closing achievement gaps they must:

- Admit they have a problem and put the data that demonstrate the problem front-and-center in a form that can be understood easily.
- Measure and report progress consistently.
- Make the goal of eliminating or narrowing gaps a priority for everyone in the organization.
- Distribute equitably resources directed toward achieving the goal.
- Implement interventions that focus on key variables early and consistently.

After discussing each of these conditions, we provide examples of how to conceptualize the combination of interventions and variables and furnish selected examples of results that reflect the reporting procedures related to the achievement gap goals featured in our strategic plan.

ORGANIZATION CONDITIONS

Reporting the Problem and the Data

Since 1998, the Arlington Public Schools has consistently proclaimed eliminating the achievement gap as a priority and has published the nature and size of the gap in relation to a number of variables. Since 1999, eliminating the achievement gap has been a goal of the district's strategic plan. Progress on the goal is measured and reported against four objectives that have been assessed according to change on 24 indicators. A quantitative target was established for each indicator for each year of the 2005–2011 plan. The objectives that support the goal include

• The achievement of Asian, Black, Hispanic, White, and low-income students, students with disabilities, and English language learners will be accelerated, and gaps in achievement will be reduced on various academic indicators and performance assessments. Indicators for this objective include gaps in
  o Percentage of students passing state criterion-referenced tests (called Standards of Learning [SOL] tests in Virginia).
  o Percentage of students reading on grade level at grades 3 and 6.
  o Percentage of students taking challenging courses, including percentage of students
    ▪ Passing Algebra 1 with a C or better by the end of grade 8.
    ▪ Enrolled in advanced courses in grades 6–12.
    ▪ Passing advanced courses in grades 6–12.
    ▪ Completing level 3 of a foreign language by the end of grade 11.
    ▪ Receiving advanced standing or credit in technical courses, earning licenses, or passing National Occupational Competency Testing Institute (NOCTI) assessments.
    ▪ Completing Advanced Placement (AP) and International Baccalaureate (IB) courses in grades 9–12 and earning qualifying scores (e.g., scores eligible for college credit).
    ▪ Passing Geometry by the end of grade 9 with a C or better.
    ▪ Passing Algebra II by end of grade 10 with a C or better.
    ▪ Earning advanced studies or IB diplomas.
  o Graduation rates, including percentage of students
    ▪ Earning a standard or advanced studies diploma.
    ▪ Graduating with any diploma.
    ▪ Graduating on time.
  o Dropout rate
  o Achievement in arts and humanities indicated by percentage of grades 6–8 students taking electives in art, music, and theater.
  o Health and wellness, including percentage of students

- Meeting or exceeding criterion levels on the Virginia Wellness-Related Fitness Tests.
- Participating in vigorous physical exercise at least five times a week as reported in the Youth Risky Behavior Survey (YRBS).
- There will be a decrease in the gaps in the proportion of APS students in identified groups participating in educational opportunities that develop their cultural knowledge, awareness, and sensitivity as measured by participation rates in foreign language classes.
- There will be a decrease in the gaps in the proportion of children completing preschool and demonstrating readiness for kindergarten as measured by the percentage of kindergarten students who were enrolled in Pre-K programs.
- There will be a decrease in the over- or under-representation in areas related to the achievement gap, including percentage of students
  o Suspended
  o Identified with disabilities
  o Identified as gifted
  o Failing courses in middle and high school
  o Retained in grade.

Measuring and Reporting Consistently

Results for these objectives and indicators are reported each year to the school board and to the public in a variety of forms. The most comprehensive report takes the form of a document that describes detailed results on all strategic plan indicators. Typically, these data for the previous school year were reported in October of the current school year at two regular school board meetings. At the first meeting in October, the report and discussion focused on results and their interpretation. The degree to which targets had been achieved for every indicator measured for which data were available at that time (typically drop-out and graduation rate data were unavailable until later in the school year) was reported in an initial document. In addition to reporting the quantitative results, a color-coded scheme was used to classify the result as reaching the target, making progress but not making the target, making no change, or moving away from the target.

At the second meeting in October, the emphasis shifted from results to recommended revisions to goals, objectives, indicators, or targets,

depending on the results achieved. For example, if targets had been exceeded in the previous year and targets previously set for the next year
had also been surpassed, the targets would be revised upward. In other instances, the data may have gone in the opposite direction from the target,
occasioning a need to adjust targets downward to keep their achievement
within the realm of the possible. A document was provided that displayed
a summary of major results.

In the example shown in Table 2.1, the report displays previous targets and results for two indicators related to gaps in enrollment in and
passing of advanced courses in grades 6–12 and the gap in the percentage of students by group enrolled in advanced courses. After all the data
were available, a final report was published in February or March that
also included a summary of changes over multiple years in the most
important measures.

In addition to this comprehensive look at progress on the achievement
gap objectives and indicators, more detailed and focused data were provided and discussed among a number of groups, ranging from faculties and
parents at a particular school to various advisory committees. For example,
in each of the past several years, the Superintendent's Advisory Committee
on Elimination of the Achievement Gap analyzed detailed data on disproportionate suspension rates for Latino and Black students, as well as data
about overrepresentation of certain groups in special education.

In some years, the focus of the group also turned to data that caused
concern in the report on the indicators for that year. In one instance, the
spotlight shone on disparities in reading scores in middle school and in
another year on disparities in enrollment in advanced classes. Other committees, consisting of parents and other residents advising on specific
curricula, analyzed gaps in achievement in science, math, or in the identification of students to receive services for the gifted.

Some reports raised concerns that required a special look at the data
beyond the summary that appeared in the strategic plan reports. Graduation rates in the 2007–2008 school year, for example, caused a level of
concern that led to the generation of a special report on that topic alone.

The point here is not to describe all of the ways in which data are
treated, but to emphasize the importance of reporting the data candidly
and emphasizing in the reporting both the good and the bad news in ways
that can be helpful to parents, the community, and the staff as they work

Table 2.1. Example of Strategic Plan Indicator Report

Goal 1—RISING ACHIEVEMENT & Goal 2—ELIMINATE THE GAP

Objective 1.2 and Objective 2.1 (B) Increase in students reading on grade level at grade 3 and grade 6

		Results					Targets		
		2003–04	2004–05	2005–06*	2006–07*	2007–08	2008–09	2009–10	2010–11
Indicator 9—Percentage of students reading on grade level on grade 6 DRP Test									
APS	No. tested	n/a	n/a	1200	1094	1117			
	Target				79	80	83	85	88
	% Reading on level	64	TBD	76	77	83			
Indicator 35—Gap in percentage of students reading on grade level on grade 6 DRP Test									
White	No. tested			581	534	581			
	% Pass			94	95	96			
Asian	No. tested			118	123	124			
	% Pass			84	80	83			
	Target Gap	n/a	n/a		18	10	7	3	0
	Actual Gap (White)	31	TBD	10	15	13			
Black	No. tested			186	157	152			
	% Pass			54	54	61			
	Target Gap	n/a	n/a		41	32	22	11	0
	Actual Gap (White)	49	TBD	40	41	35			
His-panic	No. tested			307	275	252			
	% Pass			53	55	64			
	Target Gap	n/a	n/a		44	30	20	10	0
	Actual Gap (White)	51	TBD	41	40	32			

(continued)

Table 2.1. Example of Strategic Plan Indicator Report (*continued*)

Goal 1—RISING ACHIEVEMENT & Goal 2—ELIMINATE THE GAP

Objective 1.2 and Objective 2.1 (B) Increase in students reading on grade level at grade 3 and grade 6

		Results					Targets		
		2003–04	2004–05	2005–06*	2006–07*	2007–08	2008–09	2009–10	2010–11
Disadv.	No. tested			409	360	291			
	% Pass			52	53	60			
	Target Gap	n/a	n/a		38	30	23	15	7
	Actual Gap (Non Disadv.)	TBD	TBD	36	36	30			
LEP	No. tested			429	360	264			
	% Pass			33	55	61			
	Target Gap	n/a	n/a		34	30	25	20	15
	Actual Gap (Non LEP)	TBD	TBD	29	33	28			
SWD	No. tested			159	127	140			
	% Pass			42	39	49			
	Target Gap	n/a	n/a		47	40			
	Actual Gap (Non Disabled)	TBD	TBD	39	43	38			

to eliminate the predictive power of factors such as race, income, and dominant language in determining levels of student learning.

Making Eliminating Gaps a Priority for All

While reporting the "brutal facts," as Jim Collins (2001) would suggest, represents a necessary and crucial step in eliminating achievement gaps, it is not a sufficient step. If the data are not used by all the players, the likelihood of the data changing is minimal. Organizations tend to define a problem, create a program and an office or organizational unit to address the problem, and then leave it up to that program and group of people to solve the problem, leaving the rest of the organization free of responsibility or accountability for the issue.

While that kind of approach may work with some problems, it seems to us imperative that given the breadth and depth of the achievement gap issue, the solution to that problem is the responsibility of all members of the organization. We often hear that "priorities that are the responsibility of everyone become the responsibility of no one." That may be true in some situations, but is less likely if the leadership of the organization commits to maintaining accountability for keeping the goal paramount and monitoring the accomplishment of results.

In the Arlington Public Schools, and in other school districts that address this problem seriously, narrowing achievement gaps becomes an institutional responsibility, and management systems are developed and implemented to ensure all members of the organization pay attention to the most important goals and objectives of the organization. Figure 2.1 describes in brief terms the planning and management system that guides the implementation of solutions to the issues identified as most important in the Arlington Public Schools.

The strategic plan represents the centerpiece of the system and delineates the most important priorities of the elected school board. Those priorities are reflected in the plans developed and enacted by each school and each department within the organization, consistent with their particular roles and circumstances.

The expectation is that each school's plan will address the issues of increasing achievement and eliminating achievement gaps, based on a careful assessment of the data for that school by staff and by a parent advisory group. Similarly, each administrator develops a work plan that reflects at least two of the objectives of the school or department plan related to the school district's strategic plan.

Finally, all teachers who have passed the probationary contract period assume responsibility for developing and carrying out a professional development plan aligned to the goals of the system. In that way, the quality of their work in addressing the issue becomes part of the evaluation of both administrators and teachers.

Ensuring that data are reported honestly and consistently and that all members of the organization assume responsibility for eliminating gaps in achievement become key factors in reaching the goal.

Distributing Resources Equitably

Making the goal of eliminating achievement gaps the business of everyone in the organization isn't enough. The district must allocate budget funds according to that priority to help ensure that efforts to accomplish the goal receive sufficient material and personnel support. With regard to closing the achievement gap, equitable allocation means granting ad-

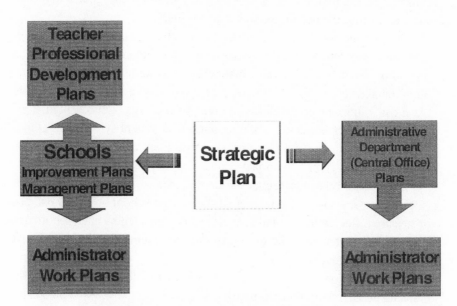

Figure 2.1   Arlington Public Schools' Planning and Management System

ditional or greater support to interventions focused on removing gaps. Schools with greater gaps in achievement should receive more resources than schools with smaller gaps.

In Arlington, for example, more resources are delivered to schools with greater needs through allocation of additional staff for English for speakers of other languages services, augmented numbers of reading teachers and services in schools with greater proportions of students eligible for subsidized meals, and more minority achievement staff and resources for schools with greater proportions of minority students. Thus, those schools receive additional resources tailored to their populations and, as a result, also tend to enjoy smaller class sizes as a function of the distribution of the extra staff. These schools also tend to receive supplementary resources through federal funds delivered under the guidelines of the federal Elementary and Secondary Education Act.

Implementing Interventions Focused on Key Variables

The final elements in creating an environment to eliminate achievement gaps are a common understanding of the key variables necessary to make progress, assurance that interventions designed for that purpose address those variables, and consistent implementation of those interventions. Again, we make no claim to having a lock on the identification of these factors, but our experience suggests at least four key variables that should undergird the development and implementation of interventions:

- Expectations
- Quality of instruction
- Access to opportunities
- Parent and community involvement.

Some of these variables overlap, particularly expectations and access to opportunities, but they represent different emphases worth maintaining as separate factors for education planning.

Expectations

By "expectations," we mean expectations of teachers, administrators, other staff, parents, and students, as well as a student's expectations for him- or herself. A large and long-standing body of research points to the important impact teacher expectations have on student achievement (e.g., Rosenthal and Jacobson 1968; Ferguson 1998, 2007). Those expectations tend to become a part of the climate or culture of the school.

When those expectations fall under the influence of conscious or unconscious assumptions about the relationship between race and achievement (Ferguson 2007; Diamond 2006; Moule 2009; Vanden Bergh 2010) they become particularly important in connection to the achievement gap. These assumptions may be shared by teachers, counselors, administrators, and other staff as well as by parents and students.

A similarly large body of research suggests the importance of expectations among students themselves for successful learning (Ferguson 2002, 2007). Research ascribes particular importance to whether students believe the locus of control for success resides within them and the effort they expend—a condition associated with increased student learning—or whether they believe it depends on chance or the influence of others— conditions associated with decreased student learning (Rotter 1989).

Interventions designed to close achievement gaps must address the variable of expectations explicitly. This includes building student confidence that they can learn well at high levels and removing from teachers and other staff members the notion of an association between race and expectations for learning, including an understanding of the impact of White privilege on such associations. (See Chapters 5–8 for a discussion of how Arlington Public Schools has addressed the issue of White privilege.)

Quality of Instruction

Expectations also affect the quality of instruction, by which we mean the quality of teaching and the quality of the relationships between instructors and students. The quality of instruction to which Arlington Public Schools subscribes is reflected in a commitment to ensuring that all students are taught for meaning, rather than subjected to instruction of discrete, isolated, basic skills or repeated rounds of remediation.

This commonsense notion that some students who do not receive instruction focused on meaning or understanding are unlikely to learn well, is reinforced by a considerable amount of research (Slavin 1987). Some of that research suggests that students taught for meaning as opposed to being taught discrete, isolated basic skills will do just as well on test items measuring basic skills, but much better on items measuring higher order skills and concepts (Knapp et al. 1995).

Teaching for meaning in this formulation includes instruction that makes connections with

- The lives of students.
- The cultures of students.
- The major concepts or big ideas of the subject taught.
- The inquiry processes of the discipline taught.
- The big ideas and the inquiry processes of other subjects taught.
- Prior instruction and future instruction.

Teaching for meaning also involves differentiated instruction conducted in a well-managed classroom environment characterized by intrinsic rather than extrinsic rewards (Smith and Knight 1997; Knight and Smith 2004). Defined this way, teaching for meaning goes a long way toward establishing the kind of classroom climate vital to nurturing supportive relationships among teachers and students.

Access to Learning Opportunities

If educators teach all students for meaning and maintain high expectations for them, the district will accomplish an important piece of ensuring that all students have access to learning opportunities. This variable also includes providing rigorous learning opportunities for students by ensuring they receive early instruction for understanding, as in pre-K experiences, and that they have access to advanced classes and receive support to learn successfully in those classes.

Parent and Community Involvement

Considerable research also suggests that the fourth major variable of interest, the support and involvement of parents and community members, can play a vital role in increasing student achievement and closing achievement gaps. (The role of community advisors is discussed in greater detail in Chapters 3–5.) As well, working with parents to teach them to help their students can pay off in increased student achievement (Epstein 1996; Ferguson 2007). School systems must consider these four variables together as they develop initiatives to close achievement gaps.

IMPLEMENTING INITIATIVES

Table 2.2 shows selected initiatives of the Arlington Public Schools intended to close achievement gaps by reference to which of these four variables constitutes the major target of the program. The major target is signified by a check with a box around it; variables addressed secondarily are designated by a check mark.

Teaching for meaning, for example, emphasizes making connections through classroom interactions, although it certainly addresses, as suggested above, the variables of expectations and access to opportunity. It does not, however, address in any substantial way parent or community involvement.

In contrast, Parents Encouraging Student Achievement (PESA) focuses almost exclusively on the variable of parent involvement, as it is designed to help parents become advocates for their children and to assist their children in their studies. Much of that encouragement, of course, addresses high expectations in a significant way.

Looking across the initiatives in this way may provide a clearer assessment of the degree to which the system addresses the variables considered most important in closing gaps and whether one or more of the variables might be neglected or overemphasized.

SELECTED RESULTS

As indicated earlier, results of efforts to close achievement gaps must be published consistently and clearly. Beginning with Table 2.3, we summarize some of the more important indicators we've tracked during the past decade. These data suggest, as indicated in the introduction, that this school district has made considerable progress on some indicators, less on others, and even on those indicators where the progress has been encouraging, the district has a long way to go.

Table 2.2. Initiatives by Variables Addressed

Initiatives	Variables			
	Expectations	Classroom Interactions	Access to Opportunity	Parent and Community Involvement
Teaching for Meaning	✓	☑	✓	
Teacher Excellence Initiative	✓	☑	✓	
Courageous Conversations	☑	✓	✓	✓
Pre-Kindergarten Programs	✓	☑	✓	✓
Full-day Kindergarten	✓	☑	✓	✓
ESOL/HILT	✓	☑	✓	✓
Title I Reading	✓	☑	✓	✓
Reading Recovery	✓	☑	✓	✓
Reading Support—Grade 6 & High School	✓	✓	☑	✓
Math Acceleration	✓	✓	☑	
SERP (MSAN)		☑	✓	
In-school Instructional Interventions (e.g., Read 180, Spell-Read P.A.T.)		☑	✓	
After School Remediation	✓	✓	☑	
Even Start Literacy	✓	✓	✓	☑
First Language Support	✓	☑	✓	✓
Teacher Expectations and Student Achievement (TESA)	☑	✓		
Early Identification Program	✓	✓	☑	✓
Pathways to the Baccalaureate	✓		☑	✓
College Summit	✓		☑	
Leadership Skills for Diversity Class	✓	☑		
Student Leadership (Latino Leadership & MSAN)	☑		✓	
Secondary Minority Achievement	✓	✓	☑	
Cohort Programs	✓		☑	
Four- and Six-Year Academic Plans	✓		✓	☑
Parents Encouraging Student Achievement (PESA)	✓			☑
Parent Academy	✓			☑

Note. ☑ = emphasized   ✓ = addressed

Standards of Learning (SOL) Assessments

Table 2.3 displays percentage passing rates on the Virginia Standards of Learning Assessments by ethnicity and total by year since the inception of the testing program. This particular display aggregates results across all grades (grade 3 through high school) and all subjects tested (English/reading, mathematics, science, and social studies). The SOL assessments are the criterion-referenced tests the state uses for its accountability system. The state also uses portions of the SOL assessments to comply with the federal No Child Left Behind (NCLB) testing requirements.

As indicated on the top section of the table, the total group's passing rate increased from 65% to 90% from the spring of 1998 to the spring of 2009. That 25 percentage point, or proportionate increase of 38%, compares to the White students' increase from 82% to 96% of 14 percentage points and a proportionate increase of 16%.

Latino students experienced a proportionate increase in passing rate of 79%, moving up 37 percentage points from 47% to 84%, while Black students more than doubled their passing rate, moving up 40 percentage points from 37% to 77%. Asian students experienced a proportionate increase of 36%, increasing their passing rate by 25 percentage points from 69% to 94%. As the table makes clear, Asian, Latino, and Black students increased their passing rate at a faster clip than White students—a necessary condition for closing the gap.

Despite these differential gains for Asian, Latino, and Black students and a consequent narrowing of the achievement gaps, a large gap in passing rates persists for Black and Latino students. The second portion of the table expresses that gap as a percentage point difference in passing rates between White students and the other student groups. The Asian student gap of 13 percentage points in 1998 declined by 85% to two percentage points in 2009. Thus, the Asian achievement gap has essentially been removed on that measure. Latino students decreased their gap with White students by 66%, from 35 to 12 percentage points, while the Black gap decreased by 58%, from 45 to 19 percentage points.

Figure 2.2 expresses the same trends in a different way, illustrating the sharper rise in passing rates for Black and Latino students than for White and Asian students and the narrowing of the gap. It also illustrates a slowing of the narrowing effect in recent years.

Table 2.3. Standards of Learning Passing Rates by Percent by Year by Ethnicity and Gaps in Passing Rates by Percentage Point Differences by Year, Ethnicity, and Total

% Passed SOL's	Year	Asian	Black	Hispanic	White	Total
	2009	94	77	84	96	90
	2008	95	74	82	96	90
	2007	93	73	79	96	88
	2006	90	72	78	95	87
	2005	93	73	82	96	89
	2004	90	70	75	96	87
	2003	89	67	74	95	85
	2002	87	63	69	93	82
	2001	82	57	66	91	78
	2000	79	50	57	89	75
	1999	73	46	52	86	71
	1998	69	37	47	82	65
% Point Gap	2009	2	19	12		
	2008	1	22	14		
	2007	3	23	17		
	2006	5	23	17		
	2005	3	23	14		
	2004	6	26	21		
	2003	6	28	21		
	2002	6	30	24		
	2001	9	34	25		
	2000	10	39	32		
	1999	13	40	34		
	1998	13	45	35		

Reading on Grade Level

The Degrees of Reading Power (DRP) is a norm-referenced reading test as opposed to the criterion-referenced Standards of Learning assessments across subjects described above. Most reading experts tout the importance of students reading on grade level by grade 3; the Arlington Public Schools has used the proportion of students reading on grade level at the end of second grade (according to the DRP measure) as an important indicator of achievement and the achievement gap.

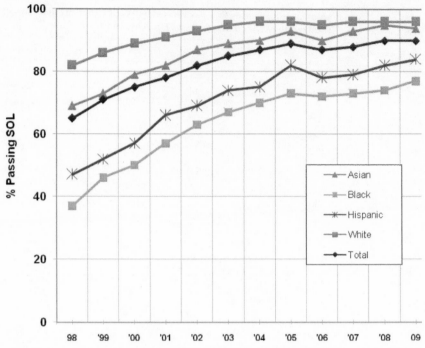

Figure 2.2   Standards of Learning (SOL) Passing Rates by Race/Ethnicity: 1998–2009

Since 1998, the district has recorded a 76% decline (from 17% to 4%) in the proportion of second graders reading below grade level at the end of grade 2—an increase from 83% to 96% reading on grade level. During that same period, the gap for Black students declined by 84% by 2008, with a gap of 14 percentage points. That gap increased in 2009 to 22 percentage points, with 76% of Black students reading on grade level compared to 98% of White students.

The gap for Latino students during that period varied greatly, a fluctuation fueled in part by variation in testing rules affecting the proportion of limited English proficient students tested. The 2009 Latino student gap was minus one percentage point, with 99% of tested Latino students reading on grade level.

The picture in grade 6 (Figure 2.3), where the same measure has been used consistently since 2003–2004, appears quite different. Middle school reading performance became a major issue among staff and advisory groups around that time, and since then the proportion of all grade 6 students reading on grade level rose by 34%, or 22 percentage points, from 64% to 86% in 2009.

The gap for Black students, from 2005–2006 to 2007–2008 decreased from 40 to 35 percentage points, or 13% with 61% of Black students reading on grade level compared to 96% of White students. Over the same time the Latino student gap decreased by 22%, from 41 to 32 percentage points, resulting in 64% reading on grade level.

These data suggest that although progress has been registered related to narrowing gaps in on-grade reading performance, much more remains to be done, particularly in the higher grades.

Enrollment and Performance in Advanced Courses

Another consistent marker used in gauging the achievement gap has been enrollment and performance in advanced courses. Since the 1997–1998 school year, the Arlington Public Schools has reported the proportion of students completing Algebra I with a C or better by the end of grade 8, recognizing the importance of early completion of Algebra I in accessing higher level mathematics and science courses in high school.

The proportion of all students completing Algebra I by grade 8 with a C or higher has risen by 127%—from 22% to 50% of the students (Figure 2.4). Using that same measure as an indicator of the achievement gap presents

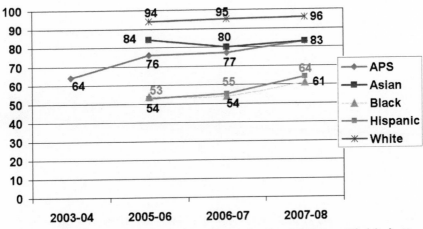

Figure 2.3   Percent of Grade 6 Students Reading on Grade Level by Race/Ethnicity by Year

a decidedly mixed picture. Black students' completion of Algebra I with a C or higher by the end of grade 8 rose by 133%, from 12% to 28% from 1997–1998 to 2008–2009. The Latino student rate of increase over the same period hit 160%, from 10% to 26% of Latino students. At the same time, the White student completion rate rose only 37%, from 52% to 71%.

Regardless of these large proportionate gains for Black and Latino students, Algebra I became the default grade 8 mathematics course for White students but not for their Latino and Black classmates. In fact, measuring the gap as the percentage point difference between the proportion of Black and Latino students completing Algebra I with a C or better by the end of grade 8 reveals an increase in the gap, despite the higher proportionate increase in the enrollment of Black and Latino students.

The Black student gap rose from 38 percentage points to 43 percentage points, and the Latino gap rose from 42 to 45 percentage points. This difference points to the finding that despite a steeper rise in the completion rate for Black and Latino students compared to White students, the increase fell short of the level needed to narrow the gap.

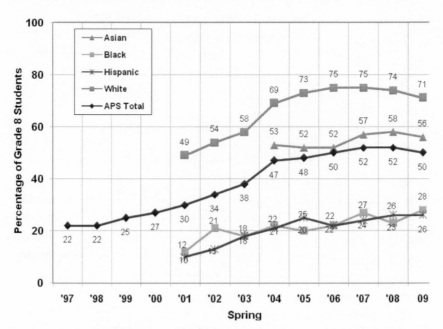

Figure 2.4   Percent of Students Passing Algebra I by the End of Grade 8 with a Grade of "C" or Better: 1997–2009

A similar trend has emerged for enrollment in advanced middle and high school classes across the board. The proportion of students enrolled in such classes has increased for all groups, with Black and Latino student enrollments increasing at a more rapid rate proportionally, but nevertheless there is a counterintuitive increase in the achievement gap.

Also, as in the Algebra I example, when performance in the advanced classes is tracked according to proportion of students passing the classes, the gap virtually disappears, despite the large racial/ethnic passing gap outside the advanced classes. Thus, although the proportion of minority students entering advanced classes has increased, they seem to pass at close to the rate of White students.

Among Latino students enrolled in advanced classes, for example, the gap in passing compared to White students has varied during the past six years by between 3 and 6 percentage points, and for Black students between 2 and 8 percentage points, with both groups within 5 percentage points of White students in 2009.

Suspension Rates

One indicator that stands out as different over the years in relation to most of the important indicators that have experienced positive, albeit less than sufficient, change is the overrepresentation of minority students among students suspended from school. Despite a good deal of attention by administrators, teachers, and advisory groups (see Chapter 4 for an account of those discussions), the gap has fluctuated for Black students during the past six years between 16 (2006–2007) and 23 percentage points (2008–2009). The Latino student gap ranged from 4 (2005–2006) to 18 (2007–2008) percentage points (table 2.4).

In the most recent year reported (2008–2009), Black students represented 13% of the population in Arlington Public Schools, but 36% of the suspensions, while Latino students represented 27% of the student population and 33% of the suspensions. The gaps between representation in the total population compared to representation in suspensions totaled 23 and 6 percentage points for Black and Latino students, respectively.

Table 2.4. Percent of Black and Latino Students Represented in the Population and among Students Suspended: 2003–2004 to 2007–2008

Indicator	2003–04	2004–05	2005–06	2006–07	2007–08	2008–09
			Black Students			
No. Students	2557	2478	2430	2345	2379	2376
% of Total Population	14	14	14	14	13	13
% of Suspensions	35	35	35	30	32	36
Gap between % of Population and % of Suspensions	21	21	21	16	19	23
			Latino Students			
No. Students	5705	5304	4866	4653	4766	4951
% of Total Population	32	30	28	27	27	27
% of Suspensions	39	37	32	40	45	33
Gap between % of Population and % of Suspensions	7	7	4	13	18	6
			White Students			
No. Students	7744	7815	7920	8160	8500	8848
% of Total Population	43	45	46	47	48	48
% of Suspensions	21	20	24	23	23	24
Gap between % of Population and % of Suspensions	22	25	22	24	25	24
			Asian Students			
No. Students	1854	1840	1806	1890	1965	1998
% of Total Population	10	11	11	11	11	11
% of Suspensions	6	8	9	8	7	7
Gap between % of Population and % of Suspensions	4	3	2	3	4	4

CONCLUSION

The data suggest that Arlington Public Schools has made progress in eliminating achievement gaps, but that we have a considerable distance to travel before we can declare that we are close to eliminating gaps based on factors such as race, ethnicity, dominant language, or income.

As will become clear in succeeding chapters, we are convinced that to make further progress we need to focus more heavily on the nexus of expectations, institutional racism, and White privilege. We also must address more explicitly the relationships among the cultural competence of staff, the expectations communicated to students, and the instructional methods employed.

In the next chapter we will address some of the approaches we have used to overcome barriers to confronting achievement gaps and move the work forward. Once again, we do not claim that this particular school district has found *the* answer, but we believe our experiences may be useful to other educators and communities.

REFERENCES

Collins, Jim. 2001. *Good to Great*. New York: Harper Collins.

Diamond, John B. 2006. "Still Separate and Unequal: Examining Race, Opportunity, and Achievement." *The Journal of Negro Education* 75: 427–505.

Epstein, Joyce L. 1996. "Perspectives and Previews on Research and Policy for School, Family, and Community Partnerships." In *Family-School Links: How Do They Affect Educational Outcomes?,* edited by A. Booth and J. F. Dunn, 209–246. Mahwah, NJ: Lawrence Erlbaum.

Ferguson, Ronald F. 1998. "Teachers' Perceptions and Expectations and the Black-White Test Score Gap." In *The Black-White Test Score Gap*, edited by Christopher Jencks and Meredith Phillips, 213–217. Washington, DC: Brookings Institution Press.

———. 2002. *What Doesn't Meet the Eye: Understanding and Addressing Racial Disparities in High-Achieving Suburban Schools*. Oak Brook, IL: North Central Regional Educational Laboratory.

———. 2007. *Toward Excellence with Equity: An Emerging Vision for Closing the Achievement Gap*. Cambridge, MA: Harvard Education Press.

Knapp, Michael S., and Associates. 1995. *Teaching for Meaning in High-Poverty Classrooms*. New York: Teachers College Press.

Knight, Stephanie L., and Robert G. Smith. 2004. "Development and Use of a Classroom Observation Instrument to Investigate Teaching for Meaning in Diverse Classrooms." In *Observational Research in U.S. Classrooms: New Approaches for Understanding Cultural and Linguistic Diversity*, edited by Hersholt C. Waxman, Roland G. Tharp, and R. Soleste Hilberg, 97–121. Cambridge: Cambridge University Press.

Moule, Jean. 2009. "Understanding Unconscious Bias and Unintentional Racism." *Phi Delta Kappan* 5: 320–326.

Rosenthal, Robert, and Lenore Jacobson. 1968. *Pygmalion in the Classroom.* New York: Holt, Rinehart and Winston.

Rotter, Julian B. 1989. "Internal Versus External Control of Reinforcement: A Case History of a Variable." *American Psychologist* 45: 489–493.

Slavin, Robert E. 1987. "Mastery Learning Reconsidered." *Review of Educational Research* 57: 175–213.

Smith, Robert G., and Stephanie L. Knight. 1997. "Collaborative Inquiry: Teacher Leadership in the Practice of Creative Intelligence." In *Reaching and Teaching All Children: Grassroots Efforts That Work*, edited by Robert S. Sinclair and Ward J. Ghory, 39–60. Thousand Oaks, CA: Corwin.

Vanden Bergh, Linda, Eddies Denesson, Lisette Hornstra, Marikus Voeten, and Rob. W. Holland. 2010. "The Implicit Prejudiced Attitudes of Teachers: Relations to Teacher Expectations and the Ethnic Achievement Gap." *American Educational Research Journal* 47: 497–527.

Chapter Three

Can Schools Eliminate Gaps?

Robert G. Smith

In the past eight or nine years it has become commonplace for school systems to adopt the goal of closing achievement gaps, yet they continue to struggle to find suitable and effective ways to achieve that goal. In the previous chapter, we discussed some focused interventions that seem, at least in some cases, to be relatively effective, but still fall far short of helping school districts eliminate achievement gaps.

Schools and school districts continue to confront a number of obstacles in their efforts to close the achievement gap. In this chapter, we discuss many of those obstacles, as well as a number of ways in which school systems might overcome them. Among those stumbling blocks are perceptions, arguments, and research findings that question the appropriateness and feasibility of reaching the goal. In some school districts, the very ways of doing business work against achieving the goal.

OWNING AND SETTING GOALS

In Chapter 2, we discussed the importance of eliminating the achievement gap as a central goal of the school system and making it the responsibility of all of the members of the organization. In Arlington, that meant the school board needed to adopt the issue as one of its most important priorities.

When the Arlington School Board first adopted quantitative objectives related to closing the achievement gap—objectives that I proposed in 1998 for purposes of our planning and management system and for the crafting of school and administrator work plans—members of the staff, the school board, the press, and the community often referred to narrowing the achievement gap as "the superintendent's goal" or "the superintendent's plan."

If the goal were identified only with me, then its realization would depend on my standing and I would be seen as having the sole responsibility for its accomplishment. Given the relatively brief tenure of superintendents and the likely duration of the problem, it was imperative that the issue *not* become the province of the superintendent alone. Similarly, it was important that solving the problem *not* be relegated to the staff or a part of the community.

During the 1997–1998 school year, we commenced work on the development of a strategic plan for the school system. Adopted by the school board in October 1999, the plan's first two goals were increasing achievement for all students and eliminating achievement gaps based on race/ethnicity. Listing increasing achievement for all students as the first goal was a considered strategy to convey the message that a focus on eliminating achievement gaps would not diminish the emphasis on raising achievement levels of all students.

The arguments leading to the adoption of the goals, and subsequent work on achieving objectives related to the goals, help illuminate the perceptions that represent some of the impediments to narrowing achievement gaps. After conducting a third-party contractor survey of Arlington parents, students, and teachers regarding strengths and weaknesses of the school system and the most important work the system should address (see Chapter 1 for examples of some of the questions asked in that and subsequent years), a school board–appointed planning committee of parents, community members, and staff began developing goals, objectives, activities, and assessments for a new strategic plan.

The issue of the achievement gap ignited the hottest fire. Many parents, staff members, and community members expressed concerns about the appropriateness of adopting closing gaps as one of the goals of the school system. Although a legitimate end, they argued, narrowing gaps based on race/ethnicity should not be the responsibility of the schools because racial/ethnic achievement disparities could be explained by social-economic status (SES) differences, and schools have neither the means nor the responsibility to change SES disparities. If apparent racial differences in student achievement could be explained by SES, goals related to racial achievement gaps would be unnecessary.

These arguments were contradicted in 1999 by analyses of Arlington SOL results, which indicated that even after controlling for SES, racial differences on achievement test results persisted. In addition, many members of the staff, the board, the community, and I countered that regardless of the influence of social and economic factors, we had a responsibility to the community to set demanding goals and that it would be an abnegation of that responsibility to ignore achievement gaps.

Through a series of events that seemed surprising at the time, the main issue related to adopting the achievement gap goal became the use of the words "narrow" or "eliminate" in relation to gaps. I recommended using "narrow" because I was concerned that the arguments of those who did not believe schools could have an impact on the achievement gap would remove the goal altogether if we proposed to "eliminate" achievement gaps. It also seemed to me that setting elimination as the goal could very well create unrealistic expectations and engender a press to adopt quantitative objectives to completely eliminate gaps during the six-year planning horizon of the plan.

In the end, proponents of the language to "eliminate" gaps prevailed, with no real public support for the more tepid "narrow." Consequently, we have set "elimination" of gaps as our goal for the past decade, both in that plan and in the Strategic Plan adopted subsequently in 2005. I chose not to continue to argue against the use of the word, and in fact appropriated it, because I believed further discussion about it would pit people against each other even if they supported the same goal. I chose, as well, to adopt the language as an important statement of our *ultimate* aim.

The issue of potentially unrealistic expectations arose again with the adoption of the second strategic plan in 2005 as the board, against the recommendation of staff but with the support of the Superintendent's Committee on Elimination of Achievement Gaps, voted to adopt quantitative targets that called for zero gaps by the end of the 2011 planning horizon on nearly all measures. The staff chose not to stand on ceremony in supporting its recommendation for more modest targets, understanding that a legitimate argument could be made that setting "stretch" objectives may lead to greater achievement.

The question of the ownership of the goals by the school board and the community receded as the school board, with community involvement, shaped and adopted the proposed strategic plan in 1999. The issue of

ownership by the school board virtually disappeared with the adoption of
the 2005–2011 version of the plan, and continuation of work on the goal
was featured prominently in the board's search for my successor, as well
as in most school board member campaigns for election.

As indicated earlier, the community, led by the school board, embraced
the goal, which took center stage in the strategic plans that were adopted
in 1999 and 2005. In both instances, the development of the plans involved approximately a year and a half of work with hundreds of community members and staff.

The development of both strategic plans began with surveys of parents,
teachers, and students. The survey samples selected for the second plan
also included community members who were not parents of schoolchil-
dren. The second survey was followed by 20 focus groups, including
additional members of the response groups, convened to help us grasp
the meaning behind the survey responses and to gather perceptions of the
most important issues on which we should work.

After the board reviewed the results and adopted tentative goals for the
plan, task groups ranging between 12 and 25 members each were assigned
to develop implementation plans that included objectives, indicators,
activities, and resources for each of the goals. The task group members
engaged parents, other community members, teachers, students, and a
number of members of various advisory groups.

The Superintendent's Advisory Committee on Eliminating Achievement Gaps, for example, played a major role in the development of the
implementation plan surrounding that goal. A Strategic Plan Steering
Committee, appointed by the board, compiled the work of the task groups
and developed a plan for the consideration of the school board. The board,
in turn, reflected on and revised the proposed plans in a retreat setting. In
both years (1999 and 2005), the board adopted the plans after considerable public comment. Undergoing this relatively inclusive deliberative
process helped build support for the goal to eliminate achievement gaps.

CAN SCHOOLS ELIMINATE GAPS?

The adoption of the goal and plan to eliminate achievement gaps essentially rejected the arguments of those who expressed concerns about

whether schools should be held responsible for eliminating achievement gaps. Although cast somewhat differently, these arguments continue today and follow a history of such discussion begun at least as early as the mid-1960s.

My perceptions about this issue also have been influenced by this history and by my experiences related to it. In 1966, when I was teaching social studies to high school students in Frederick County, Maryland, James Coleman of Johns Hopkins University and his associates published a landmark study of American education titled *Equality of Educational Opportunity*. Among other things, Coleman and his associates concluded that only 10% of the difference in student achievement could be explained by school-related factors such as per-pupil spending or level of teachers' education. Among minority students, the explained variance doubled to 20%. Other factors, such as SES or level of parents' education, carried greater explanatory value.

Given these findings and later studies, such as analyses published by Jencks and others (1972), it became a common argument that schools should focus on those things schools can control, and that the effects of class and race are largely impervious to school intervention. As a teacher and school administrator during those years, I believed the finding might be accurate given current conditions, but that teachers, parents, and communities could change the gloomy conclusions by better and more focused instruction.

In succeeding years, a number of educational researchers concentrated their work on the processes of instruction, finding that changes in teaching could result in changes in student achievement for all students (Brophy and Good 1986), supporting and giving hope to those of us in education who saw examples every day of where we believed we were making a difference.

More recent analyses by Richard Rothstein (2004) sound a note similar to those of Coleman and Jencks. Arguing that school-related factors can, at most, explain about 40% of the variance in student achievement outcomes, Rothstein suggests that educators set themselves up for failure by setting eliminating gaps as the goal.

Granting that schools can have an impact and praising the progress of some, Rothstein suggests that a series of social measures designed to reduce gaps among students from different social classes may be more effective and less expensive than educational interventions to reduce gaps. In fact, he argues that until social class disparities are attacked and removed, we cannot expect to eliminate gaps.

Among the measures he suggests are increased minimum wage, labor relations reforms directed at increasing the incomes of low-paid workers, a commitment to low unemployment, subsidized housing for poor families, and school-community clinics. He also recommends adopting education-related reforms that go beyond current school reform efforts, including major expansion of early childhood education, after-school programs, and summer programs.

In a 2009 policy paper, David Berliner expressed concern that the focus of No Child Left Behind (NCLB), which set the year 2014 as the time when achievement gaps would disappear through a regimen of testing and sanctions, unfairly assigns sole responsibility for overcoming achievement gaps to schools and unjustly indicts schools for failing to eliminate them. He reviewed the powerful impact of what he terms out-of-school factors, largely related to poverty.

While acknowledging some responsibility for schools to help narrow gaps, Berliner, like Rothstein, prescribes a much more comprehensive agenda than does NCLB. For example, he cites the need to address, as a society, issues such as reducing the incidence of low-birth-weight children, providing high quality pre-K education for all children, and instituting universal medical care.

In recent discussions with school and community groups regarding the achievement gap, school system staff and advisory group members have reviewed progress over the years (see Chapter 2), noted the apparent slowing of progress on some measures, and despite general improvement in minority student achievement, noted movement toward a greater gap on others. Also injected into the discussion have been the issues of how much progress schools can bring about and the findings of the kinds of studies cited above.

At the same time, it is of note that during the past 40 years, using the results from Coleman et al. (1966) and Rothstein (2004), the reported variance in achievement outcomes explained by school factors has at least doubled. Does this increase simply reflect more precise and sophisticated measurement or does it argue that schools have become more effective in reducing gaps predicted by societal factors? The answer probably lies somewhere between these two propositions. Demonstrable progress has been recorded, and it appears that schools *can* improve on the results already achieved.

We do not contest the estimates of the amount of variance in student learning explained by educational factors, but view those estimates as status reports rather than conclusions about the limits of educational influences. That is, we perceive those estimates to represent a current reading of the power of educational factors to explain or predict student achievement as opposed to a ceiling on their effects.

At the same time, we make no claim of knowing the outer limits of the influence of educational factors and recognize that our educational treatments may not be strong enough to overcome *entirely* the kinds of factors cited by Rothstein, Berliner, and others. Eliminating achievement gaps—removing the predictive power of factors such as race/ethnicity, income, and dominant language on student achievement—will likely take a coordinated social effort that features, but goes beyond, school factors and functions.

Recognizing and acknowledging that the influence of educational treatments may be limited creates a double-edged sword. On the one hand it could lead to arguments that would relieve education and educators of the responsibility to eliminate achievement gaps. In the absence of such potential or responsibility, the argument to transfer resources from education to other social measures would be bolstered.

On the other hand, acknowledging potential limits of educational interventions and the importance of other factors could lead to setting more realistic expectations for education, moving away from blaming schools for achievement deficiencies and working toward a cooperative venture across social agencies, including education, to eliminate achievement gaps. Within that framework, educators must seek to increase the impact of their educational initiatives while acknowledging the importance of increasing the efforts of the larger society to reduce the impact of factors on achievement over which the schools can exercise little control and which educational treatments may not be able to counter or vanquish.

As we argued in Chapter 2, responsibility for eliminating achievement gaps should be shared across the entire school system rather than be assigned only to a special office or a series of special projects. In this chapter we conclude that elimination of achievement gaps should be a central, preeminent societal goal, but not the sole responsibility of schools. Just as educators should not be "let off the hook" by attributing the gap to only social factors, communities should not be exempted from their responsibility by making the closing of gaps exclusively the mission of schools.

BUILDING ON STRENGTHS AND SUCCESS

These questions regarding the intersection of class, race, and the responsibilities of schools and other social agencies cut across many of the perceptions that represent barriers to advancing the work of eliminating achievement gaps.

In Chapter 2, we outlined four variables that we believe need to be addressed if we are to make progress on this issue: expectations, quality of instruction, access to opportunity, and parent and community involvement. Progress on all of these variables depends on the work of classroom teachers and on the allocation of resources.

Turning first to the work of teachers, it is important to note that the progress detailed in Chapter 2 is attributable in large measure to the work of teachers and the instructional and administrative personnel who help them. If teachers, principals, instructional supervisors and specialists, and counselors do not expect students of color to do as well as other students, then the quality and rigor of the instruction and services directed toward those students will suffer, the students' access to opportunities for advanced educational experiences will be diminished, and the messages to parents will be less positive.

One of the themes played out over the years across many school districts has been reserving for White, middle-class students the opportunity to engage in rigorous courses (Mathews 1998). Arlington Public Schools shared that tendency.

Shortly after adopting the goal of eliminating achievement gaps in 1999, APS had a complex network of prerequisites, including teacher recommendations, that governed whether students could enroll in rigorous classes. After engaging in many conversations with Black and Latino parents who recounted stories of pressuring teachers and administrators to allow their children to try Algebra I in grade 8, or to enter other putative advanced classes, I became convinced that we needed to make major changes in our gate-keeping procedures for advanced courses if we hoped to change their composition from mostly White to a mosaic more representative of our total student population.

Generally, according to the stories of rejection I heard, the teacher, counselor, or principal would suggest that the child had not performed on prerequisite course work to a level that would portend success in grade 8 Algebra I, and that the school would not want to set the student up for failure or force the teacher to "water down" the class. In a number of instances, persistent badgering by the parents led to the students' entry into Algebra I despite the prerequisites. In these cases the students typically succeeded.

In response, procedures for entry into advanced classes as outlined in programs of studies and school handbooks were revised with the help of central staff, principals, and teachers. Parents were told that if they wanted their children to try an advanced class they could do so, with the understanding that the standards for those classes would be maintained.

White and minority parents had complained about the barriers to enrollment in advanced classes, but the perception among minority parents was that when White parents protested, they were heard. Many parents also perceived that White parents were more likely to raise objections to the course entry procedures. Thus, while the changes designed to allow students the opportunity to engage in rigorous course work may have been motivated by achievement gap issues, they were embraced by and benefited the children of many parents, minority and majority.

These changes were augmented by overt attempts by principals, counselors, and teachers to encourage minority students and solicit the support of their parents to enroll them in rigorous middle and high school courses.

One high school principal, for example, asked teachers to identify students of color who had not been enrolled in advanced classes but who the teachers believed could be successful in such courses. The principal accumulated a robust list of students and met with each one to encourage him or her to attempt at least one Advanced Placement class. The effort paid off in a marked increase in minority student enrollments in advanced classes by the following school year.

Even with the large increases in the proportion of minority students entering advanced classes, student achievement in the advanced classes overall remained about the same, and one achievement gap, as measured by the proportion of students passing advanced courses, was barely in evidence (see Chapter 2).

As more students who previously would not have been involved in advanced classes participated in more rigorous course work, the nature of the conversation among Arlington educators began to shift. Rather than expressing concerns about lowering of standards, teachers reported to colleagues the successes students experienced and the ways in which they and their colleagues would adjust their instruction to enable that success.

Principals and counselors shared ways in which they would identify students who were not engaged in advanced course work but who they believed could be successful, and encouraged them to try such classes. As reports of student success increased, the feasibility of the procedure and of the more general goal became increasingly credible.

In short, success bred more success, resulting in school climates much like those characterized by Hoy, Tarter, and Hoy (2006) as having high levels of academic optimism. In these schools, the components of collective efficacy (the faculty's belief that it can exert a major impact on student learning), trust (the faculty's confidence that teachers, parents, and students can work together to improve student learning), and academic emphasis (a school's press for student success) are mutually reinforcing in encouraging and achieving student academic success.

Sharing such successes became a centerpiece of the collaborative professional development among teachers within school faculties, within subject/level meetings, and across the entire school district. In one high school, for example, teacher study team deliberations led to the development of what became a very successful initiative to increase the enrollment and support the success of minority males in Advanced Placement classes. Students were identified and invited to join a "cohort" of like students who met weekly with two or three faculty members with the intent of preparing for and succeeding in Advanced Placement classes.

When this approach began in 1999–2000, 15 males of color were represented in 21 AP classes. By 2008–2009, 85 males of color in the cohort were taking 161 AP courses. Black students, representing 29% of the school's enrollment, made up about 20% of the AP enrollment. Latino students, constituting 44% of the school's enrollment, were 40% of the AP enrollment. The emphasis on working with a particular cohort was expanded after the initial success to include a school-wide emphasis on preparation for rigorous courses.

Across the school system, teachers were expected to develop professional development plans as part of the teacher evaluation system. Many of those plans addressed issues related to closing achievement gaps. Each year, teachers met at a convocation to report on the results of their classroom research. Then, as now, concerns surface from time to time regarding the goal of eliminating gaps and the likelihood of reaching it.

Some of these conversations center on reserving the privilege of enrollment in advanced classes to "truly" advanced students. The proportion of all students enrolled in such classes in grades 9–12 in a given year has risen to more than 40%, and the proportion of students graduating from high school having completed one or more Advanced Placement (AP) or International Baccalaureate (IB) classes during their years in high school has risen to 75% of the class, prompting concerns by some students, parents, and teachers that the entry of so many "unprepared" students into advanced classes diminishes the quality of the experience for those who are better prepared.

These conversations intensified in 2008, when all four Arlington high schools were ranked in the top one-half of 1% of the nation's high schools on Jay Mathews Challenge Index in *Newsweek Magazine*. However, the fact that student performance on the AP and IB tests had not noticeably declined with the increase in participation vitiated the complaint.

Another related issue that arises more from certain community and parent interests than from staff, has to do with perceived conflicts between working on issues related to achievement gaps as opposed to other priorities. As indicated in Chapter 1, the vast majority of Arlington parents, community members, and teachers believe we can work on eliminating achievement gaps while maintaining high standards for all children. Nevertheless, when the district is considering allocation of resources, questions surface periodically about whether the emphasis on closing achievement gaps works to the disadvantage of more advantaged populations (e.g., majority students, gifted students, native English language speakers).

This issue often arose at superintendent "chats" during the past few years. At these gatherings, typically hosted by parents who invited neighbors to their home, the arguments by those concerned about the diversion of resources from their interests to eliminating the achievement gap have been blunted by a relatively liberal stance on the issue by the general community and by demonstration by the school district that student achievement across the board is on the rise.

The most recent context in which that issue played out originated, somewhat surprisingly, with members of the Superintendent's Advisory Committee on Eliminating Achievement Gaps. The members of the group protested the school board's budget adoption for the 2009–2010 school year, which expanded elementary foreign language programs in a year when revenues were down, enrollments were up, and the superintendent's proposed budget recommended no program expansions.

The committee members argued that rather than expanding elementary foreign language opportunities, the board should allocate those resources to overcoming achievement gaps. The board stuck to its budget proposal, but because of a change in the state funding formula for pre-K initiatives, was able to expand pre-K classes (a priority of the committee) without committing any more local funds, and could therefore argue that it had balanced the allocation of funds to a program viewed by members of the committee as an interest of more advantaged populations.

STALLED PROGRESS AND CULTURAL COMPETENCE

Many of these questions regarding self-interest and privilege swirl around discussions about an observed slowing of the progress on narrowing gaps nationally (Magnuson and Waldfogel 2008) and locally. These discussions between Whites and minorities about the too slow narrowing of the achievement gap tend to return to the issues of expectations and access to opportunity. These issues affected by elements of institutional racism are reflected in the perceptions, perhaps unwittingly or unconsciously, of an overwhelmingly White administration and faculty (see Chapter 1).

I came to believe, and the school district leaders agreed, that the issue of "cultural competence" and the subset of issues related to White privilege must be confronted directly, systematically, and over time if we hoped to continue the progress we enjoyed on narrowing gaps in the early years. My personal participation about five years ago in a community Seeking Educational Equity and Diversity (SEED) group, led by coauthors Palma

Strand and Marty Swaim and populated by a racially and nationally diverse group of parents and staff, helped crystallize this perspective.

I vividly remember a senior staff meeting a few years ago at which coauthor Alvin Crawley reported on the deliberations of the staff group he was leading (see Chapter 8). Alvin described his conviction, shared by members of the Cultural Competence Council, that although our faculty and staff may be well meaning, the messages many of them convey to students and their colleagues are colored by White privilege and work against our mutually held goal. (See Chapter 4 for additional discussion of White privilege.)

I became convinced that Alvin and the Cultural Competence Council were right and that the school district must launch a serious and sustained effort to change the messages. Succeeding chapters chronicle much of that work, its antecedents, and its effects.

THE IMPORTANCE OF ALLIES

In addressing this issue and the other concerns described earlier, we have found the identification of and work with allies who can provide moral, political, social, and intellectual support to the effort to be helpful. Included among those allies are school groups, community groups, other school district representatives, and scholars. Two school-related groups that have helped our efforts include the Superintendent's Advisory Committee on Eliminating Achievement Gaps and the Superintendent's Advisory Committee on Accountability and Evaluation.

When I first took the position of superintendent in Arlington, school board members and key community members gave me the names of a number of people they believed would be helpful in addressing achievement gap issues. I met with this group, comprised primarily of Black community members and parents, one Saturday a month to listen to its members' concerns regarding the approaches the school district had taken in the past and the approaches they recommended for the future. For whatever reason, these meetings turned into group diatribes against the Arlington school system and the Arlington community. I believed I was being held responsible for the perceived trespasses of prior administrations and for an immediate turnaround in practices and perceptions. I ultimately disbanded the group because it represented too few parents, seemed mired in past disappointments, and perhaps caused me too much discomfort.

Despite that personal distress, I learned much from those prickly sessions about the depth of bitterness suffusing the history of desegregation in Arlington and the negative perception key opinion leaders in the minority community had of school personnel. I also learned a number of valuable lessons about how to frame achievement gap issues.

For example, one member of the group taught me that focusing on the achievement gap could diminish the accomplishments of a large number of minority students who achieve at high levels. It is a lesson that I have taken to heart and it prompted me to stress to faculty and community groups that minority youngsters are among our top scholars.

I replaced that initial group with an advisory committee that included parents and staff. For the past decade, this committee has provided constructive advice on ways to eliminate achievement gaps. That advice and the committee's advocacy made a considerable difference in our approaches to various interventions to improve staff development, student counseling and education planning, parent involvement, and student discipline. (See Chapters 4 and 5 for discussion of the group's work.)

Similarly, the committee that helped us address issues of accountability and evaluation provided guidance on the assessment of programs that have attempted to narrow gaps, ranging from English Language Arts to the work of the Office of Minority Achievement. The committee also played a central role in developing the community satisfaction surveys referenced in Chapter 1.

Other school committees that advise the school board also have become allies in this work, including the Advisory Committee on Instruction (ACI), which reports to the school board, and some of the subject area advisory committees that work through the ACI. Among community groups, we have found allies in the National Association for the Advancement of Colored People (NAACP), the League of United Latin American Citizens (LULAC), the Civic Coalition for Minority Affairs, and the county government's Commission on Human Relations, which have supported and challenged us.

Outside the school system, we found valuable professional development allies in the Mid-Atlantic Equity Center and the National Multi-Cultural

Institute. The National Multi-Cultural Institute also helped us by conduct-ing an equity audit of our organization (see Chapter 8).

We also sought allies among school districts across the country with the formation of the Minority Student Achievement Network in 1999. Initially, Allan Alson, the superintendent of the Evanston Township High School District in Evanston, Illinois, contacted the superintendents of 15 other diverse, mostly inner-ring suburban school districts, inviting them to attend a meeting during the American Association of School Administra-tors (AASA) annual conference, held that year in New Orleans. Out of the 15 superintendents, 14 attended the session facilitated by Bob Peterkin of Harvard's Graduate School of Education.

All of the districts shared a goal of eliminating achievement gaps. They also generally shared small- to moderate-sized enrollments, a sub-urban location, diverse populations, recognized and published achieve-ment gaps by race and ethnicity, good financial resources and support, and strong relations with one or more institutions of higher education. A number of the districts were located in university communities such as Amherst, Massachusetts; Ann Arbor, Michigan; Berkeley, California; Cambridge, Massachusetts; Chapel Hill, North Carolina; Evanston, Il-linois; and Madison, Wisconsin.

All 14 superintendents agreed to join together to form the Minority Student Achievement Network (MSAN) and held their first annual confer-ence that spring in Evanston. The organization has now grown to 25 school districts with an executive director and offices associated with and located at the University of Wisconsin–Madison Center for Educational Research.

The major purpose of the organization was to discover, investigate, and implement principles and practices likely to take race and ethnicity out of the student achievement equation. The thinking of the superintendents was that their organization should set a research agenda and collaborate with scholars who shared those interests. If they could not make substan-tial progress given their commitments, their resources, and the help of renowned scholars, what school district could?

Edmund Gordon, then with the College Board, assembled an initial advi-sory committee of scholars. While that particular committee did not persist, it provided an initial forum for the cultivation of university scholar allies who have helped advance the research agenda, the professional develop-ment efforts, and the student development initiatives of member districts.

Among the distinguished scholars who have supported MSAN are Bob Peterkin, Ron Ferguson, and John Diamond from Harvard; Gloria Ladson-Billings from the University of Wisconsin–Madison; Wade Boykin from Howard University; Pedro Noguera from New York University; Uri Treisman from the University of Texas, Austin; and Suzanne Donovan, Executive Director of the Strategic Education Research Partnership (SERP) Institute.

The structure of the organization includes a governing board comprised of the member district superintendents and a research-practitioner council consisting of two or three educators from each district. The governing board members set policy for and conduct the business of the organization, and share their work in narrowing achievement gaps. The research-practitioner council carries out the research agenda, which currently focuses on mathematics, literacy, teacher-student relationships, and conversations about race.

In addition to conducting annual conferences, teacher-research sessions, and a number of professional development mini-conferences devoted to selected topics, the organization also sponsored an annual student conference. The student conference provided a forum for students of color to come together to discuss hurdles to achievement for minority students and develop plans to help reduce achievement gaps to take back to their school districts (MSAN 2009). Arlington teachers, administrators, and students have participated in these activities and the school system has hosted a number of the conferences over the years.

Working with all of these allies helps cement the importance of the goals and assists the school district in working through the difficult and sometimes contentious conversations in this arena. In the absence of such allies, it will be difficult to initiate the cooperative efforts with the community and other social agencies that we believe will be required to spur further progress on closing gaps. In succeeding chapters we address the difficult work of implementing measures to engender cultural competence within the organization and the community.

LESSONS LEARNED

What have we learned throughout this journey that will help us create conditions for success?

Establish Necessary Organization Conditions and Address Major Variables

We described and provided examples in Chapter 2 of the prerequisite organization conditions for making progress toward this goal. Establishing these conditions, we discovered during implementation of our strategies to close achievement gaps, was more productive than blaming parents, teachers, or students. Those conditions included

- Acknowledging the problem and putting the data that demonstrate it front and center.
- Measuring and reporting the problem consistently.
- Making the goal a priority for everyone in the system.
- Distributing equitably resources directed toward accomplishing the goal.
- Implementing interventions that focus on key variables that must be addressed to reduce the gap.

The four variables that must be addressed by interventions are

- Expectations of teachers, parents, community members, and students that all students will learn to high levels.
- Quality of instruction, including teaching methods and the relationships established in the classroom.
- Access to rigorous educational opportunities.
- Parent and community involvement and support.

We have learned that we must continue to pay attention to, maintain, and improve on these organization conditions and continue to focus on these variables in attacking achievement gaps.

Apply Principles Rather Than Replicate Procedures

We learned from repeated programming efforts that it is the application of principles rather than the replication of the details of programs implemented elsewhere that will allow us to make progress. Although we learn from colleagues elsewhere, the ways in which we implement interventions must be based on our local conditions, our needs, and our strengths.

Our experiences with implementing staff development and instructional programs, described in detail in succeeding chapters, demonstrate that we will be more successful if we capture the principles of efforts proven effective elsewhere and adapt the procedures to local conditions. That is, we learn from others, but make the staff development or instructional interventions fit our own conditions.

Good Intentions Are Insufficient

Good intentions are certainly necessary to making progress, but are insufficient to reach the goal. Those good intentions must be married to knowledge of the principles that must be implemented, provision of the necessary resources, and persistence in the face of adversity and failure.

Build on Strengths

The examples of program interventions referenced in Chapter 2 and professional development efforts described in Chapters 4–8 demonstrate clearly that we make progress when we build on strengths and allow one success to inform the next, rather than attack real or imagined deficits or attack people rather than problems.

Recruit Allies

Throughout this book, we illustrate the importance of support from others, from the base of community sentiment committed to eliminating achievement gaps to the advice provided by experts and the resources and expertise furnished by other social agencies. While schools can make progress and should be held responsible for doing so, this problem is too big and too important for schools to handle alone. New forms of cooperation need to be invented and pursued.

Confront Race

As we reflected on the relationships between cultural competence, White privilege, and student achievement, we became convinced that achievement gaps will remain large and progress halting unless we directly confront the issue of race in ways that allow all of us to understand the impact of our own race on the problem. Changes in instructional interventions and the application of resources may impel considerable progress, but gaps will remain until hearts and minds also change. We have a far distance to go as an organization and as a community in making that kind of change.

Miles to Go

The achievement gap persists as the most important challenge facing American education, and we have miles to go on this journey, but we are confident that given the resources and the commitment from schools, communities, and other social institutions, we will overcome it. We have learned that we can make substantial progress in narrowing achievement gaps through interventions that intentionally focus on specified variables.

We have also come to understand that while we can make more progress, we will be slowed down if we do not confront directly the host of issues and expectations captured by the term "White privilege," and if we assume that education and educators are solely responsible for making progress on the elimination of achievement gaps. We must work with our allies, including our students, parents, and the larger community, to make elimination of achievement gaps a reality.

REFERENCES

AP Network. 2007. *The Wakefield High School AP Network: Building Bridges to Your Student's Future.* Retrieved August 2009 from http://www2.apsva.us/APNetworkBrochure2007-08.pdf

Berliner, David C. 2009. *Poverty and Potential: Out-of-School Factors and School Success.* Boulder, CO, and Tempe, AZ: Education and the Public Interest Center & Education Policy Research Unit. Retrieved April 2009 from http://epicpolicy.org/publication/poverty-and-potential

Brophy, Jere, and Thomas Good. 1986. "Teacher Behavior and Student Achievement." In *Handbook of Research on Teaching*, 3rd ed., edited by Merlin C. Wittrock, 328–375. New York: Macmillan.

Coleman, James S., E. Q. Campbell, C. J. Hobson, J. McPartland, A. M. Mood, F. D. Weinfeld, et al. 1966. *Equality of Educational Opportunity.* Washington, DC: U.S. Government Printing Office.

Hoy, Wayne C., John Tarter, and Anita Woolfolk Hoy. 2006. "Academic Optimism of Schools: A Force for Student Achievement." *American Educational Research Journal* 43: 425–446.

Jencks, Christopher, et al. 1972. *Inequality: A Reassessment of the Effect of Family and Schooling in America*. New York: Basic Books.

Magnuson, Katherine, and Jane Waldfogel, eds. 2008. *Steady Gains and Stalled Progress: Inequality and the Black-White Test Score Gap*. New York: Russell Sage Foundation.

Mathews, Jay. 1998. *Class Struggle: What's Wrong (and Right) with America's Best Public High Schools*. New York: Three Rivers Press.

Minority Student Achievement Network (MSAN). 2009. *Overview*. Madison: Wisconsin Center for Education Research. Retrieved August 2008 from http://msan.wcerw.org;about/index.aspx

Newsweek Magazine. 2008. "Top of the Class 2008: The Complete List of the 1300 Top U.S. High Schools." Retrieved July 2000 from http://www.newsweek.com/id/39380

Rothstein, Richard. 2004. *Class and Schools: Using Social, Economic, and Educational Reform to Close the Black-White Achievement Gap*. Washington, DC: Economic Policy Institute.

Chapter Four

Fixing the System, Not the Kids

Palma Strand

In the prior two chapters, Rob Smith shared his superintendent's perspective and focused on the demographics of the system as a whole. He summarized foundational steps that school systems as organizations must take to make progress in closing achievement gaps. And he identified some internal and external factors that have affected the quest.

In his discussion, Rob refers to a turning point at which key actors realized that strong policies were not enough, that changes in institutional culture were necessary, and that those changes would only occur by transforming individuals' behavior throughout the system. The chapters that follow this one describe in depth a primary initiative—cultural competence training—that APS has undertaken to accomplish these transformations and how that training is being taken to scale within the system.

This chapter details the basis for concluding that cultural competence training will address the institutional racism that we believe is a significant contributor to achievement gaps. Then, after introducing the essentials of that training, the chapter uses a systems approach to explain how changing individual attitudes and actions will change institutional culture, which is necessary for changing institutional outcomes.

EDUCATION AND THE DEEP INEQUALITIES OF RACE

It is close to 20 years since my oldest child headed off to kindergarten in the Arlington Public Schools. My youngest child graduated from APS in

2009. I now teach in another state. Why am I still committed to the project that is this book? The most immediate reason is the urgency of transforming public education so achievement gaps disappear.

But education is only one of many areas in which deep inequalities related to race continue to be evident in this country. In my professional work in law, the problem of how to address continuing racial disparities arises in many different contexts. Legal doctrine focuses on identifiable discriminatory acts, particularly those by individuals. Most of the time, intent is required; sometimes effect is enough.

Many if not most racial disparities today, however, do not result from specific, identifiable acts. They are instead the product of multiple acts by many individuals in various institutional contexts. Yet racial inequality remains. The question arises: Should such inequality be outside the reach of the law?

Critical Race Theorists have provided insights into the phenomenon of continuing racism defined structurally. They direct our attention to social structures and institutions, to the concept of institutional racism. As Cheryl Robinson describes in Chapter 5, they offer us insights such as the need for counter-stories, the social construction and embeddedness of race, and the myth of equal opportunity.

What Critical Race Theory lacks is an explanation of how systems work, of how these various threads wind together to form the cord that is institutional racism. Critical Race Theory is also short on concrete examples in which the operation of institutional racism is tracked in an actual system. Our case study of the APS work on achievement gaps offers an explanation and provides an example.

In this chapter, I trace how the new science of complex adaptive systems provides insight into the process through which racially disparate results such as achievement gaps emerge from social systems and institutions such as schools. I then explain, from a systems view, why the APS cultural competence training works to reverse institutional racism in a school system setting. Finally, I discuss specific aspects of the APS cultural competence training from a systems perspective.

LOW EXPECTATIONS AND ACHIEVEMENT GAPS

"Those kids." I can't remember the first time I heard someone say those words, but I can remember the first time I really understood what I was hearing. I was talking to the principal of the elementary school one of my children attended, and the conversation had to do with proposed program changes at the school that were designed in large part to do better by the school's Black and Latino students. In two words, he set "those kids" apart and dismissed them.

I was still new: new to the school and new to the concerns of equity that were the subject of our conversation. And I certainly was new to any ability to not just recognize this sort of coded comment—White principal to White parent—but flag it and challenge it, especially in a constructive way. I said nothing, but afterward I stewed about it and stored it away.

So when the issue of low expectations for Black and Latino students came up for discussion at the Superintendent's Advisory Committee on the Elimination of the Achievement Gap, of which I was a member, I had a concrete sense of what that abstract term means. It is a "those kids" attitude, and it can be explicit, implicit, or buried so deep that the person with the low expectations doesn't even know he or she has them.

As the Harvard implicit bias test affirms,[1] we are socially conditioned not just to see but also to attach value to race. From an early age, we are far from "color blind" (Bronson and Merryman 2009), although we may be "color mute" (Pollock 2005). Code terms such as "those kids" are often as close as we, White folks in particular, get to actual race talk.

Fairly early on, APS identified low expectations for minority students as a primary cause of achievement gaps. Teachers and other school personnel communicate their expectations to students, and students often adjust their behavior, self-image, and achievement to those expectations. These expectations are communicated in many different ways.

Two examples of expectations that the Superintendent's Advisory Committee discussed are (1) classroom interactions such as the questions posed to and wait time allowed for various students to respond and (2) school recommendations as to the types and levels of courses—more or less challenging—that students will take.

With the first example, less thought-provoking questions let students know that teachers believe them incapable of grappling with difficult material, and shorter wait times indicate a teacher's assumption that a child is not worth investing class time in because he or she will not be able to formulate a solid response.

With the second example, when guidance counselors advise middle school students that they don't need to start the foreign language study necessary for an advanced high school diploma (the norm for college-bound students) or when math teachers steer students toward eighth grade math instead of Algebra I or regular Algebra I instead of intensified Algebra (which in APS covers more material in more depth) or when Advanced Placement or International Baccalaureate courses are not considered in high school, the message conveyed to students is that the adults in the school don't expect them to excel.

To address issues of expectations in classroom interactions, APS began offering Teacher Expectations/Student Achievement (TESA) training for teachers in 1987. TESA is a program that modifies teacher expectations by modifying teacher behavior. It prescribes specific teacher behaviors— such as addressing challenging questions to and ensuring equal wait times for all students[2]—that have been found to elicit superior responses and better outcomes for minority students.

When teachers use the TESA techniques, minority students perform better, teachers' expectations improve, and a "virtuous cycle" results: Teachers' attitudes change because they see their minority students in a new light, with new possibility. These new attitudes and higher expectations reinforce positive student responses.

Similarly, starting sometime in the late 1980s or early 1990s, APS began preparing four- or six-year academic plans for minority students in some schools to improve minority student access to higher-level courses. These plans were initially used by Office of Minority Achievement coordinators working with Black students and their families in some of Arlington's middle and high schools. Their goal was to have more of those students take the "building block" and then the capstone courses necessary for success in high school and beyond.

Both of these initiatives started on a small scale within the system— TESA as a volunteer-only training opportunity and the academic plans only for students in schools with minority achievement coordinators. APS staff tracked both programs and determined they demonstrated positive results. In the early 2000s, the advisory committee then worked with staff to expand both initiatives in the system. Since that time, TESA training has expanded substantially, although it is not yet required for all APS teachers.[3] Six-year academic plans are now mandatory for all secondary school students, and they have been adopted as an indicator of the implementation of strategic plan goals.

Effective though these initiatives were determined to be, they were indirect in terms of changing *expectations*—the "those kids" attitude. TESA alters teacher behavior, which elicits changes in student performance, which then shift teacher experience and thus expectations. The six-year plans steer minority students to rigorous courses and academic achievement; when teachers see more minority students enrolling and succeeding in higher-level courses, their expectations change for the better.

What was missing was an effort to address head-on the attitudes and awareness of the adults who were interacting with the students. Why not try to transform teachers' and counselors' expectations of minority students directly as well as indirectly? After all, wouldn't TESA techniques be even more effective if teachers were concurrently examining their unarticulated but perhaps detrimental assumptions about the kids they teach? And wouldn't six-year plans be more likely to be a meaningful exercise if counselors were challenging themselves to consider what they see as the likely path for minority students?

Moreover, as work on achievement gaps progressed, APS identified some consistent manifestations of low expectations for which no clear counter-strategies existed. For example, APS staff, the advisory committee, and the county's Human Rights Commission began looking closely at disaggregated data on school suspensions and referrals to special education—especially the referral of Black boys and the interpretation of the "least restrictive environment" requirement in the preparation of Individual Education Plans (IEPs).

These examinations showed that minority students were suspended disproportionately often and that the skew occurred in suspensions based on subjective standards such as "insubordination." Similarly, minority students were disproportionately identified as needing special education and recommended for more restrictive settings. Given the high level of subjectivity inherent in all these determinations, the data strongly suggested the relevance of differential expectations.

But what changes should follow from these realizations? One response might be to change the criteria for suspensions or develop stricter standards for special education referrals and IEPs. The fundamental challenge, however, is that schools run on thousands upon thousands of individualized relationships and everyday interactions. There must be room for individual discretion and variation, which makes the "best practice" in any situation hard to prescribe.

How, for example, should a teacher respond when a particular Latina student consistently fails to bring in her homework? How should an assistant principal interact with posturing Black boys in the middle school hallway? What assumptions should a teaching team make when a child's parents do not appear for parent-teacher conferences? Should a teacher who encounters a Black child who is loud and antsy conclude that the child is "trouble" or that she is "bright and bored"?

A handful of people—administrators, minority achievement staff, members of the advisory committee, and teachers—began to explore the idea of challenging low expectations for minority students directly. This approach would complement and enhance rather than replace the behavior-based approaches such as TESA and the six-year plan: Those initiatives would more likely lead to higher expectations if teachers and other school personnel were concurrently reflecting on their expectations. Further, this approach could reach interactions such as suspensions and special education decisions for which no clear programmatic initiatives appeared to exist.

CULTURAL COMPETENCE TRAINING TO ADDRESS LOW EXPECTATIONS

This exploration coalesced into the APS initiative on "cultural competence": the attainment of "attitudes, skills, behaviors, and policies" that enable those within the school system to develop positive relationships and "work effectively in cross-cultural situations."[4] The initiative's focus is on the interpersonal: It acknowledges that many or most of us do not currently know but can learn how to interact constructively with those from other cultures.

The relevance of cultural competence to achievement gaps is the conviction that low academic expectations by adults in schools are a major contributor to low achievement. Moreover, this cause lies unequivocally within the control of teachers and other school personnel, a majority of whom are White and middle class. These adults may lack the ability to work effectively with students of other backgrounds, and they are likely to fail to understand the power dynamics of race within schools. These deficiencies create a "vicious cycle" of low expectations and poor academic outcomes in which low expectations elicit poor outcomes, which reinforce the original low expectations, and so on.

The APS cultural competence training begins with enabling people to traverse cultural, ethnic, racial, and class boundaries. Although the term "competence" is used, the training makes clear that cultural competence involves a highly sophisticated set of skills that can always be extended or deepened or nuanced. As those of us who have facilitated cultural competence training are the first to admit, we are all on this journey, which means that cultural competence training is more like journeying toward a horizon than to a definitive destination.

Along with these cultural navigation skills, APS cultural competence training reveals the need for intentional and active awareness of and challenges to relationships and attitudes of power and privilege that advantage or disadvantage people according to their culture, ethnicity, race, or class. Teachers and other school personnel must understand not only their own and other identities and cultures, but also the power dynamic that ensconces White middle-class culture as the unquestioned norm in schools while marginalizing other cultures.

For example, schools may rely on individualistic and competitive modes of learning or indirect disciplinary commands that are in tension with Black culture (Boykin, Lilja, and Tyler 2004; Delpit 1995). When the culture of schools and the power dynamic within schools are made visible, teachers and other personnel can see how students from backgrounds other than the White middle class may feel alien rather than mainstream, fugitive rather than embraced (Hudson 1999).

Because there is a dominant culture in schools, a culture that reflects the dominant culture of society, one task must be to enable all students to become proficient in that culture—it is the culture of power and success. Emphasizing respect for students' own cultures while they are taught proficiency in the dominant culture, however, is an essential aspect of communicating the respect for who they are and their inherent ability that forms the basis for high expectations. Anti-"ism" training, which illuminates the role of race in maintaining privilege and power, is thus an indispensable part of the APS cultural competence training.

This exposure of and challenge to underlying issues of power and privilege is perhaps the most difficult component of transforming an institutionally racist system and the most sensitive aspect of the APS cultural competence training.[5] In our dominant (White middle-class) culture, certain assumptions are common but unstated. As mentioned previously, Black or Latino boys may trigger a presumption of danger or violence, and the older they are the stronger the presumption. Parents who miss conferences may be presumed to lack concern for their children's education. We may see highly active Black or Latino children as behaving improperly rather than not sufficiently challenged academically.

Similarly, certain code words or phrases are often used to communicate low expectations without spelling out the message. In my first example, "those kids"—as well as "those parents" or "that school"—when uttered by one White person to another in reference to Black or Latino children, parents, or a school with a predominantly minority population, are red flags: The speaker is invoking a shared experience of Whiteness that need not be stated but that sets "us" apart from and above "them."

White people are conditioned by the hierarchy of racial politics and the learned experience of Whiteness to let these statements go. Whiteness is in large part about not noticing and not asserting the obvious. Too often, we who are White hear such coded statements and allow ourselves to be drawn into complicity through silence even when we do not agree.

The APS cultural competence training addresses the culture and privilege hierarchy indirectly through an emphasis on stories and directly through instruction in conducting difficult conversations. The APS training uses at least three different types of stories: stories from films and books, stories in the form of the narratives of guest speakers, and personal stories shared by group members with each other. Even though some members of our team were skeptical of the use of stories at the outset (especially those of personal experiences), a trial-and-error approach led us to incorporate them into the work.

Stories are a direct mode of accessing people's common humanity, and they reach people's hearts in a way that makes the "head" work of cultural competence training much more compelling. But they also put people on the same footing and strip away differences of power and privilege. This is true whether the stories are told by those who lack or those who have privilege, whether they are stories of hurt and anger or stories of dawning awareness and breaking the silence of racial privilege.

More directly, instruction in difficult conversations enables people to challenge racial hierarchy. Difficult conversations training, used in conversations about race, gives people tools and approaches to counter not only directly discriminatory or prejudicial statements or actions, but also unstated or coded ones.

The first step in difficult conversations work is to not let things pass. But most people are not comfortable with confrontation and conflict and often do not think well on their feet, especially when confronted with a racially loaded comment. So the second step is to not assume that because you did not say something at the time of the incident it is over and done with. This gives one the opportunity to consider various options for approaching the person and raising the subject.

A variety of techniques fit multiple contexts. Is the person someone with whom you have a continuing relationship? Where is the other person in relation to you in the power hierarchy? Sometimes asking a question of genuine interest makes sense: "What did you mean the other day when you referred to 'those kids'?" or "You've pointed out this problem with parents not attending this kind of school function. Do you have any ideas for what causes that or where to go from here?" or "I've heard you state a concern that we shouldn't place minority kids in academically challenging classes because we don't want them to fail. Why do you think they will fail and what do you think we can do to prevent it?"

Sometimes sharing a personal experience makes sense: "One of my kids went to that school, and that was her best school experience ever! What do you see as the problems with it?" or "I've found that restless kids are often the smartest kids in the class. Do you think the material is engaging and challenging them?"

Thinking about these conversations and even rehearsing them beforehand makes tangible the challenge to power and privilege included in the APS cultural competence training. People need to have options for how to act. Inviting people to be "change agents" without giving them tools doesn't take the work as far as it needs to go. When I look back on the conversation with my child's principal with which I started this chapter, I recognize that today I would have the ability to not just let his reference to "those kids" slide but to develop a response that would invite reflection rather than put him on the defensive.[6]

CULTURAL COMPETENCE, INSTITUTIONAL RACISM, AND SYSTEMIC CHANGE

In various discussions of institutional racism, cultural competence is the suggested remedy (Cross 1988; Hanssen 1998; Better 2002). At first blush, this seems paradoxical: How can attention to individual attitudes and interactions address systemic, institutional racism? The answer lies in an understanding of systems.

The key insight of institutional racism is that it is a system of advantage associated with institutional practices rather than discrete actions of personal prejudice (Tatum 1997). But institutional practices are, by definition, simply what the people in an institution do (Helmke and Levitsky 2006). And in schools, what people do is interact: The school day is nonstop relationships and interactions. *Institutional racism in schools can thus be defined as individual interactions that embody low expectations and elicit poor outcomes, achievement gaps, which are then accepted and ratified by other interactions.*

When a teacher with a lack of cultural competence and low expectations for minority students designs class activities that fail to engage those students and at which they perform poorly (pedagogy that is likely to be accompanied by similar acts that also communicate low expectations) and when this poor outcome becomes the reason these students are not placed in higher-level classes, that's institutional racism. Individualized "intent" to discriminate may not be present, but discriminatory outcomes emerge nonetheless.

A school district such as APS can be understood as a complex adaptive system, an approach that is increasingly being applied to business organizations (Clippinger 1999; Lewin and Regine 2000, 2001).[7] Complex adaptive systems consist of individual actors interacting in ways that lead to the emergence of a discernible pattern at the system level. The relationship between the individual behavior and the system-level pattern is not linear, and the individual behavior is not dictated by a system-level coordinator, which renders such a system "self-organizing" (Waldrop 1992; Johnson 2001).[8]

In a business complex adaptive system, the successes and failures of the firm emerge from the interactions of the firm's employees and customers. And, counter to many conventional business notions, there is a rising sense that businesses that focus first on employees, then on customers, and last on shareholders ultimately do better than those that focus first on shareholders, then on customers, and last on employees (Lewin and Regine 2000, 2001; Pascale, Milleman, and Gioja 2001).

Such success results from empowerment that gives employees the ability to adapt and innovate and enables the organization to evolve and change to best meet its mission under ever-changing conditions. Where the individuals in a complex adaptive system share an overall goal but have maximum discretion as to how to further it, the individual interactions will self-organize to that end.

Although a school district's mission is education rather than profit, it has the same complex adaptive system characteristics as a for-profit firm: The system-level results depend on the relationships and interactions of the individuals within it, including students. *Changing a system-level result such as achievement gaps, therefore, will require changing individual interactions and relationships throughout the entire system.*

It is, after all, in classrooms, hallways, and on the playground before, during, and after school that kids experience school—whether they feel anonymous and disregarded and likely to fail or known and respected and likely to succeed. This view is entirely consistent with initiatives such as TESA and six-year plans, which are designed to change decentralized interactions directly. This view also illuminates the contribution of cultural competence training, which seeks to transform relationships and interactions by changing attitudes and developing understanding (Marion 2006).

The complex adaptive systems view is also consistent with an increasing body of work that focuses on preventing system failure in contexts that range from airplane cockpits to hospital operating rooms (Dekker 2007). Here, studies increasingly reveal that most system failures are cumulative rather than the result of a single large blunder. They are the culmination of multiple errors, no one of which would have itself caused the adverse outcome (Gladwell 2008; Pronovost and Vohr 2010).[9]

In these contexts, moreover, an important contributing factor in preventing system failure has been flattening the hierarchy that exists within the system. Thus, for example, equalizing the power differential between pilots and copilots has led to fewer plane crashes (Gladwell 2008). Similar measures in hospitals have led to better medical results (Dreifus 2010). The common thread is that when more people feel empowered to bring a problem to the attention of the group, fewer missteps are likely to pass uncorrected. More watching eyes keep everyone on their toes.

From this perspective, the crux of cultural competence training is that it transforms individual interactions, changing them from those that comprise institutional racism, unthinking but nonetheless devastating "those kids" interactions. It does so by helping adults in schools recognize attitudes that are so deeply ingrained that they have become second nature.

With awareness comes the potential for change. Whatever society we grow up in, we have "tapes in our heads"—stories about the world that play whenever we encounter relevant people or situations. Often we don't even know these tapes are playing. Cultural competence training provides the impetus, the space, and the time to begin to acknowledge those tapes and then to start the long, slow work of countering them and replacing them with new tapes or recording over them.

None of us will ever erase the tapes we have, given the lives we have led and the stories we have heard, but we can overlay different melodies and rhythms on them.[10] When cultural competence guides us to "our kids" tapes and transforms relationships and interactions accordingly, discrimination at the system level—institutional racism—diminishes. From a complex adaptive systems perspective, the pattern that emerges at the system level from transformed individual interactions and relationships literally is reformed.

KEY ASPECTS OF A SYSTEMIC
CULTURAL COMPETENCE APPROACH

As it has grown and evolved, the APS cultural competence training has manifested a systems approach in several key ways. First, it has slowly but steadily expanded within the Department of Instruction. It started with volunteer staff and community members, then expanded to administrators, then to school board members and teacher trainers. Now those teacher trainers are being trained to train the broader pool of teachers.

At each step there are those who "get it" and are transformed, those who are neutral, and those who actively resist. This is to be expected. Not everyone will move at the same pace. But the cultural competence training energizes those who will be enthusiastic "evangelists" and exposes those who are cautious but will grow more receptive over time.

More than anything else, the approach acknowledges that this is not a short-term project; it is a long-term shift in the very culture of the institution from one that expects and allows achievement gaps to one that does not. Its localized beginnings, however, testify to the kind of innovation that grows within and eventually has the capacity to change complex adaptive systems.

Second, the APS cultural competence training evolved with contributions from many outside sources. Rather than importing a "ready-made" training curriculum, APS melded elements of diversity training designed specifically for education, facilitation and dialogue skills training, use of literature and other sources, and personal conversation and stories. As compared to an off-the-shelf curriculum, developing the training in-house allowed that training to be tailored to APS's population and needs.

More important, this development from within increased the buy-in of those in the system who were directly responsible for creating it. The APS cultural competence curriculum is *our* curriculum—Cheryl Robinson's, Tim Cotman's, Alvin Crawley's, Marty Swaim's, mine. We can look at it and see which pieces were contributed and by whom. This gives us an investment in it far greater than we would have in a pre-packaged curriculum. We are, after all, teachers. This growth from within initiated by people in the system is, again, typical of a complex adaptive system.

Third, for several years there was an annual community cultural competence discussion group consisting of 10 to 12 parents and community members with some school personnel folded in. Participants included presidents of the County Council of PTAs, the Superintendent, the Assistant Superintendent for Instruction, other parents, and a few teachers and other school personnel. More recently, a separate training for school board members has been undertaken.

APS also has sponsored community forums for parents and other community members to come and express their feelings and concerns on issues related to achievement gaps. Though small in scale, these efforts reflect an awareness that the system that is APS exists within the larger system of Arlington County. One characteristic of complex adaptive systems is that they are often nested within other systems (Csermely 2006).

Unlike other communities, Arlington has not undertaken an in-depth community-wide discourse on race and race relations—historically or in the present.[11] Many believe that there are important unresolved hurts and conflicts and acts of power and privilege in Arlington, past and present, that surface in the schools—among school personnel, between families and schools. At some time in the future a broader-based dialogue may be seen as useful by those in a position to initiate and support it. Until then, the more limited APS initiatives stand as placeholders.

Finally, a systems view illuminates the value of diversity within the organization (Hamel 2009).[12] In a complex adaptive system, innovation and resilience are inherent in different local populations adapting to different local conditions. One of the strengths of a systems view is that it recognizes the value in innovation at the local level—innovation that may eventually be useful in other locales.

Ideally, individuals in the system's various schools will respond to the APS cultural competence training by fashioning initiatives that address their own specific needs and concerns. These should look different in high schools versus middle schools versus elementary schools and schools that are majority minority versus majority White. Other variations in demographics such as older versus younger teaching populations or different principals having different strengths and agendas will also affect the specifics of school responses. Across the board, these individual innovations require time and space within schools for teachers and others to observe, talk, brainstorm, and plan.

One of the most successful APS initiatives related to achievement gaps to date—an initiative at Wakefield High School, where the "cohort project" brings male Black and Latino students together to support each other to succeed—resulted when a principal gave her staff time and space to think about how achievement gaps were manifesting themselves in their school and to plan ways to address them.

The program has evolved over time not only in response to staff observations but in response to the students. For example, while initially the program temporarily excluded students whose grades had slipped, the students asserted that the program was most important precisely when and for students who had stumbled. The program's facilitators listened and revised the program, which resulted in deeper student buy-in.

Decentralized initiatives such as this, which will facilitate greater transformation throughout the system, are most effective when they are part of an overall organizational initiative (Guinier and Minow 2007).[13] One way to achieve this is through top-level policies that make closing achievement gaps an APS priority; another is through support for system-wide initiatives such as TESA, six-year plans, and cultural competence work.

Another important centralized practice is data collection. Data are collected not just on achievement *per se* but on other performance measures that APS has slowly but surely incorporated into what it views as indicators of the system's health. These indicators include information on suspensions and special education referrals, but also more fine-grained studies such as reviews of teachers' comments on report cards to see if there are racial disparities.

The provision of time not only for cultural competence training but for follow-on work is essential yet often overlooked or undersupported. This is work that takes time, and teachers in general have very little of that commodity (Swaim and Swaim 1999).

What leaders in a complex adaptive system can do, then, is facilitate articulation of the mission, development of protocols, and provision of resources (financial, training, and other). Most importantly, they must nurture innovation and welcome disparate contributions (Hamel 2009). What the individuals throughout the system in various schools can do is to bring that sense of mission to everything they do, every interaction with students, parents, and fellow school personnel.

It is in these everyday individual actions that cultural competence training operates to shift an institutionally racist system to one in which students receive an education that is not color-blind or color-mute, but in which expectations are high—not just in word but in deed—for all kids. But cultural competence "change agents" will be far more effective if their work is supported by the organization as a whole.

LESSONS LEARNED

Looking at my experiences with APS and its efforts to reduce achievement gaps overall, I see that the perspectives I have gained fall into three essential categories, which reflect the three roles in which I have interacted with the school system in working on this challenge: (1) parent of a child or children in the system; (2) parent/community member looking at the system overall; and (3) first trainee and later facilitator in APS cultural competence initiatives. And so I present my Lessons Learned in three groups.

First, as a parent working with and representing other parents, my Lessons Learned are:

- Parents and other adults should be invited to contribute what they can (and asked what they can contribute) rather than blamed for what they can't or don't. Parents want the best for their children. Parents should be invited to give their views, and they should be listened to. Their experiences of the school system represent priceless information about how schools interact with kids.
- Often the best way to elicit nonracist behavior is to explicitly articulate positive expectations. Assume the best of people and tell them what that best is. Most people want to be fair; people work in and with public schools because they care about kids. Adults, like children, will generally meet the expectations that are communicated to them—when those expectations are clearly articulated.

Second, as a community member who served on the Superintendent's Advisory Committee and in strategic planning processes, my Lessons Learned are:

- For systemic change, it is useful to provide multiple forums for people in different roles to talk to each other about achievement gaps, institutional racism, and cultural competence. These forums create spaces in which people can listen, learn, and ultimately grow and from which innovation and creativity emerge.[14]
- For systemic change, it's valuable to create a continuing organization (such as the Superintendent's Advisory Committee) whose job is to push the issue, to ask questions, to suggest initiatives and directions. There also must be accountability to this body in that it receives data and responses and reasons.

Third, as a trainee and facilitator in the area of cultural competence, my Lessons Learned are:

- The issue of race in particular must be raised explicitly by facilitators. People are so fearful—Blacks of being hurt; Whites of saying the wrong thing and being viewed as racist—that they will not put race on the table, and it can all too easily remain the elephant in the room. Turning the light on is a necessary first step.
- Once that first step is taken, an environment that is safe but uncomfortable is necessary for forward movement. If the environment is not safe, people will shut down and dig in. If it is not uncomfortable, the impetus for change, learning, and growth is absent.
- This means that facilitation skills are important. It is not enough to train people in the substance of antiracism and give them groups to run. Process is key (especially when dealing with sensitive issues such as race), and while some people will have natural aptitude or prior experience, the necessary expertise must be ensured through training.
- Stories, stories, stories. Stories are the best way to bridge social fault lines—race, ethnicity, religion, socioeconomics, institutional role, religion. Stories give people access to each other's humanity.
- People need concrete tools for changing their behavior or to help them develop their own. Difficult conversations, organizing techniques, and instructional practices are examples.

NOTES

1. A description of the Implicit Association Test (IAT) can be found at www.projectimplicit.net/. To take the test, go to www.understandingprejudice.org.

2. There are 15 recommended TESA behaviors grouped into three categories (http://lacoe.edu/includes/template/document_frame.cfm?toURL=documents&id=8124&OrgID=165 [retrieved August 31, 2010]):

- *Response Opportunities*—Equitable Distribution of Response Opportunity; Individual Help; Latency; Delving; and Higher-Level Questioning
- *Feedback*—Affirming or Correcting; Praise; Reasons for Praise; Listening; and Accepting Feelings
- *Personal Regard*—Proximity; Courtesy; Personal Interest and Compliments; Touching; and Desist

3. APS also offers PESA introduction training for parents. "First offered to APS parents during the 2002–2003 school year, PESA is a parent education pro-

gram modeled after the TESA (Teacher Expectations and Student Achievement) program. A group of 15 to 20 parents meet once a week for 6 consecutive weeks in order to discuss interactions designed to demonstrate high expectations for their children. PESA training is facilitated by parents who have attended a two-day trainer-of-trainers workshop. The PESA program emphasizes the importance of the influence of the child's first teacher, the parent, and provides strategies for improved communication and strengthened relationships. The interactions coincide with those highlighted in TESA training. This enables parents and teachers to send the same message of high expectations to students" (www.apsva .us/1540108310840780/blank/browse.asp?A=383&BMDRN=2000&BCOB=0& C=54945#pesa [retrieved August 31, 2010]).

4. APS defines cultural competence as follows: "Cultural competence is a set of attitudes, skills, behaviors, and policies that enable organizations, such as the Arlington Public Schools, and staff to work effectively in cross-cultural situations. It reflects the ability to acquire and use knowledge, beliefs, attitudes, practices and communication patterns of others to improve services, strengthen programs, increase community participation, and close the gaps in a given area relative to the status among diverse populations. Simply stated, cultural competence is the level of knowledge-based skills required to work effectively with persons from particular groups" (www.arlington.k12.va.us/15401017133533887/site/default.asp?1540 101713353387Nav=/&NodeID=1503 [retrieved August 31, 2010])

5. Another, more familiar type of hierarchy common to schools can also work to inhibit progress on achievement gaps: School systems are, by and large, highly hierarchical overall, and this hierarchy is reproduced within individual schools. In addition, teachers are often isolated and for the most part have enormous autonomy within their classrooms—not so much over what is taught (because content is heavily determined by the testing requirements of No Child Left Behind via the Virginia Standards of Learning [SOL] standardized tests and applicable APS curricula) as over how they teach and the relationships they establish with their students. In this kind of environment, it may be difficult to encourage a culture in which people observe and question the behavior that tends to perpetuate achievement gaps.

6. The other obvious tool relates to different instructional "best practices," discussed in Chapters 6 and 7.

7. Similar approaches can be found in Ori Brafman and Rod A. Beckstrom, *The Starfish and the Spider: The Unstoppable Power of Leaderless Organizations* (New York: Portfolio, 2006) and Dee Hock, *Birth of the Chaordic Age* (San Francisco: Berrett-Koehler, 1999).

8. Examples of complex adaptive systems cross traditional disciplinary lines and appear in biology (bird flocks, ant colonies, firefly synchrony), social

science (cities, societies, and economies), neurology and psychology (human consciousness), and law. See Johnson (2001); Waldrop (1992) (various examples); Michael Batty, *Cities and Complexity: Understanding Cities with Cellular Automata, Agent-Based Models, and Fractals* (Cambridge, MA: MIT Press, 2005) (cities); Jane Jacobs, *The Death and Life of Great American Cities* (New York: Random House, 1961) (cities); R. Keith Sawyer, *Social Emergence: Societies as Complex Systems* (New York: Cambridge University Press, 2005) (human societies with an emphasis on communication); Adam Smith, *The Wealth of Nations Book IV* (Amherst, NY: Prometheus Books, 1991) (1776) (economies described in "invisible hand" terms); Olaf Sporns, *Networks of the Brain* (Cambridge, MA: MIT Press, 2010) (neurological networks and consciousness); Harold J. Morowitz and Jerome Singer, eds., *The Mind, The Brain, and Complex Adaptive Systems* (Santa Fe Institute Studies in the Sciences of Complexity Proceedings) (Boulder, CO: Westview, 1994) (neurology and human consciousness); Palma Joy Strand, "Law as Story: A Civic Concept of Law (with Constitutional Illustrations)," *Southern California Interdisciplinary Law Journal* 18 (2009): 603 (law).

9. "The typical [plane crash] involves seven consecutive human errors" (Gladwell 2008, p. 184).

10. I think of this as similar to a "mash up" in music—a composition that's made up of two or more songs in which the tracks are laid one atop the other. The original tape or composition will always be there, but now other melodies, rhythms, or vocals can also be heard.

11. In 2008, Arlington County held a series of "Diversity Dialogues" designed to facilitate conversation among disparate groups in the community. Several follow-up steps have since been taken. See www.arlingtonva.us/portals/topics/diversity_dialogues.aspx (retrieved August 31, 2010). Note that these conversations were framed in terms of "diversity" rather than "race" and/or other specific types of diversity.

12. Hamel also endorses empowering employees and flattening organizational power hierarchies (Hamel 2009).

13. "Organizational catalysts work best if they exist within and are already tied to the institution rather than superimposed from the outside" (Guinier and Minow 2007, p. 272).

14. Examples in the APS initiative are the Superintendent's Advisory Committee on the Elimination of the Achievement Gap, the Council on Cultural Competence for APS employees, the Strategic Plan Task Group on Cultural Competence, Community "SEED" (Seeking Educational Equity and Diversity) Cultural Competence Groups, and Parent Conversations Convened by the Advisory Committee and the Office of Minority Achievement.

REFERENCES

Better, Shirley Jean. 2002. *Institutional Racism: A Primer on Theory and Strategies for Social Change*. Lanham, MD: Rowman & Littlefield.

Boykin, Wade, Amy J. Lilja, and Kenneth M. Tyler. 2004. "The Influence of Communal vs. Individual Learning Conduct on the Academic Performance in Social Studies of African-American 4th and 5th Grade Children." *Learning Environments Research Journal* 7: 227–244.

Bronson, Po, and Ashley Merryman. 2009. *Nurture Shock*. New York: Grand Central.

Clippinger, John Henry, III, ed. 1999. *The Biology of Business: Decoding the Natural Laws of Enterprise*. San Francisco: Jossey-Bass.

Cross, Terry L. 1988. "Cultural Competence Continuum." *Focal Point*. The Bulletin of the Research and Training Center on Family Support and Children's Mental Health, Portland State University, Fall 1988.

Csermely, Peter. 2006. *Weak Links: Stabilizers of Complex Systems from Proteins to Social Networks*. Berlin/Heidelberg, Germany: Springer.

Dekker, Sidney. 2007. *Just Culture: Balancing Safety and Accountability*. Aldershot, UK: Ashgate.

Delpit, Lisa. 1995. *Other People's Children: Cultural Conflict in the Classroom*. New York: New Press.

Dreifus, Claudia. "A Conversation with Dr. Peter J. Pronovost: Doctor Leads Quest for Safer Ways to Care for Patients." *New York Times*, March 8, 2010. Retrieved October 22, 2010, from http://www.nytimes.com/2010/03/09/science/09conv.html

Gladwell, Malcolm. 2008. *Outliers: The Story of Success*. New York: Little, Brown.

Guinier, Lani, and Martha Minow. 2007. "Dynamism, Not Just Diversity." *Harvard Journal of Law and Gender* 30: 269, 272.

Hamel, Gary. 2009. "Moon Shots for Management." *Harvard Business Review* 87: 91–98.

Hanssen, Evelyn. 1998. "A White Teacher Reflects on Institutional Racism." *Phi Delta Kappan* 79: 694–698.

Helmke, Gretchen, and Steven Levitsky, eds. 2006. *Informal Institutions and Democracy: Lessons from Latin America*. Baltimore: Johns Hopkins University Press.

Hudson, Mark. 1999. "Education for Change: Henry Giroux and Transformative Critical Pedagogy." *Against the Current* 83. Retrieved October 20, 2010, from http://www.solidarity- us.org/node/1734

Johnson, Steven. 2001. *Emergence: The Connected Lives of Ants, Brains, Cities, and Software*. New York: Touchstone.

Lewin, Roger, and Birute Regine. 2000/2001. *Weaving Complexity and Business: Engaging the Soul at Work.* New York: Texere.

Marion, Russ. 2006. "Complexity in Organizations: A Paradigm Shift." *Studies in Fuzziness and Soft Computing* 6: 247–269.

Pascale, Richard, Mark Milleman, and Linda Gioja. 2001. *Surfing the Edge of Chaos: The Laws of Nature and the New Laws of Business.* New York: Cross Business.

Pollock, Mica. 2005. *Colormute: Race Talk Dilemmas in an American School.* Princeton, NJ: Princeton University Press.

Pronovost, Peter J., and Eric Vohr. 2010. *Safe Patients, Smart Hospitals: How One Doctor's Checklist Can Help Us Change Health Care from the Inside Out.* New York: Hudson Street Press.

Swaim, Marty Schollenberger, and Stephen C. Swaim. 1999. *Teacher Time: Why Teacher Workload and School Management Matter to Each Student in Our Public Schools.* Arlington, VA: Redbud Books.

Tatum, Beverly Daniel. 1997. *Why Are All the Black Kids Sitting Together in the Cafeteria? And Other Conversations about Race: A Psychologist Explains the Development of Racial Identity.* New York: Basic Books.

Waldrop, M. Mitchell. 1992. *Complexity: The Emerging Science at the Edge of Order and Chaos.* New York: Touchstone.

Chapter Five

Capitalizing on Synergy

Cheryl Robinson

This chapter includes vignettes that identify the need for our work, a rationale for the importance of talking about race, and an explanation of Critical Race Theory. The chapter continues with a discussion about the elements of the process Arlington Public Schools used to create an infrastructure that supports systemic professional development, focusing on the relationship between race and student achievement, ending with the lessons learned along the way.

Most people desire change; however, few realize the process, time investment, and intentionality required to create movement within an established system. Setting the stage for systemic change requires capitalizing on synergy.

Vignette 1—The Drop-out Committee determines if the district has a problem, and if so, what needs to be done to reduce the number of Black and Latino children who leave school without a high school diploma.

Vignette 2—The Overrepresentation Committee convenes to determine ways to reduce the disproportionate number of Black male students identified for more restrictive placements on the special education continuum.

Vignette 3—The Mathematics Committee meets to discuss the huge disparity between the test scores, grades, and enrollment patterns among students who are White, Black, and Latino.

Vignette 4—The Graduation Committee establishes strategies to meet the needs of students who are not likely to graduate because they have not successfully passed mandated tests.

Vignette 5—A parent group meets to discuss the continued outrage and
frustration relative to their children's lack of success and the school
district's inability to meet their children's academic, social, and emotional needs.

What do all these vignettes have in common? Each focuses on solving
long-standing symptoms of problems in the educational system rather
than on the root causes of those problems. Each seeks a "quick fix" for
the students and their families rather than solutions that focus on the institutional challenges that are at the root of the problem.

Many of the persons involved in these vignettes believe that seeing,
acknowledging, or talking about race is politically incorrect or impolite.
Some believe that race is no longer a challenge and that racism does
not exist. Others are miseducated and unaware of the struggles African
Americans, Native Americans, Asian Americans, and South and Central
Americans have endured during their quest for civil rights in America.
The majority has never thought about what it means to be White in a place
where Whiteness is not only favored and revered, but influences every
institutional structure.

Many of the remedies designed to eradicate disparities in education
have used a deficit model, which blames the victims of inequities for their
current condition, sometimes focusing on life experiences, culture, and
ways of existing as the sole culprit or source of the results. Examples of
deficit model remedies in education include:

• Providing programs that teach parents how to operate within the school
  system rather than focusing on the information educators need to know
  and actions they need to take to make connections with families and
  include their voice in the education process.
• Creating after-school, pull-out, and academic support programs for
  students on Saturdays rather than providing professional development to prepare teachers to provide appropriate instruction during
  the school day that addresses each student's talents, interests, and
  challenges.
• Designing alternative programs for students rather than creating inclusive environments where administrators and staff are required to meet
  the needs of students with diverse learning styles and needs.

Solutions based on the deficit model generally enable failed systems to remain in place, provide remedies that do not last, and offer answers that do not serve the best interests of children. In the few instances where such programs are effective, they are limited in size and in scope and are unavailable to other children who are equally capable and deserving.

In contrast, models that focus on behaviors that schools can control and that empower staff to work successfully with students are more likely to yield long-lasting and sustainable changes. Creating awareness about the core of any issue is the first step in creating solutions. Discussions must begin with a clear intention and a mutual agreement about the definitions of the terms that will guide the work. Shared definitions help people who may have different beliefs or perspectives develop a mutual understanding. Therefore, this section begins with definitions of race and racism.

WHY TALK ABOUT RACE?

Race is a socially constructed means of control that perpetuates social, political, psychological, religious, ideological, and legal systems of inequity (Smedley and Smedley 2005). Racism is also the systematic mistreatment and subordination of a certain racial or ethnic group based on skin color or other physical characteristics. Racism can also occur when systems of advantage are put into place based on the belief that one set of characteristics is superior to another set. *Racism is not always intentional.* Racist acts can be the result of the conscious or unconscious biases of individuals.

From its inception, the United States has elevated the culture and experiences of one group of people (Whites) over the life experiences, customs, and values of other racial groups. Native Americans were the first to experience domination resulting from White privilege, and it continues to affect their experiences as well as the experiences of people of African, Latino, and Asian descent.

Racism is responsible for the disproportionate number of people of color who are poor. Racism affects housing (Smith and Stovall 2008; Feagin 1999; Massey 2005; Yinger 1998), health care (Smedley and Smedley 2005; Randall 2002; Coello, Casanas and Rocco 2004), earning power, and wealth distribution (Conley 2001); and all of these factors have an impact on education. In fact, racism is pervasive and influences all institutional systems. It is so deeply entrenched in American society that most people, particularly those who are White, do not understand that it is the reason for many societal challenges.

The children described in the scenarios at the beginning of this chapter are primarily Black and Latino. Yet, the discussions designed to offer remedies to race-based problems rarely include the concept of race. The dialogue also omits a focus on the ways perceptions affect student success.

Perhaps these oversights occur because people are not aware of the relationship between race and learning. Without conversations that focus on ethnocentrism, White privilege, or perceptions of race as the foundation for the symptoms to which educators react daily in classrooms, on playgrounds, and in meetings, the goal of eliminating race as a predictor of achievement will continue to fall short of its target.

Before adult behavior can change, individuals must be aware of the impact living in a racist society has on each of us. This awareness includes acknowledging the existence of privilege and its relationship to oppression. Then educators can examine their personal views about race and the ways perceptions and beliefs affect educational outcomes for students. Educators cannot serve children effectively until this personal work occurs.

The work rests on three important premises:

1. Privileges based on racial classification do exist.
2. The result of living in a society where unequal treatments exist is that each of us develops unconscious biases.
3. Once unconscious biases are uncovered or acknowledged, opportunities to reflect and test new tools and strategies emerge, resulting in the creation of successful teaching and learning environments.

CRITICAL RACE THEORY IN EDUCATION

The beginning of the discourse about the pervasive impact of race on social structures in America is in the works of Frederick T. Douglass (1890) and W. E. B. Du Bois (1897), which described the role of race in the plight of African Americans. Derrick Bell and others began to apply ideas about how deeply Whiteness is entrenched in American society and the way group dominance leads to differential experiences (Delgado and Stefanic 2000). Bell studied the impact of "racialized" experiences relative to legislative appointments, enactments of laws, severity of sentencing, and myriad decisions and behaviors within the legal field. This body of work, known as Critical Race Theory (CRT), applies to other disciplines and explains the ways in which race is a social construct.

A social construct is an idea that may appear to be natural and obvious, but in reality is a creation of a particular culture. Gender, race, wealth, and religion are examples of social constructs, and the concepts described in CRT apply not only to the experiences of racial groups (Yosso 2005; Delgado and Stefanic 2001) but also to disenfranchised groups such as immigrants (Romero 2003) and women (Bernier and Rocco 2003).

CRT identifies characteristics that lead to institutional racism or the notion that Whiteness and assimilation are the goals to which all others must aspire. The CRT framework offers five powerful ideas that can inform conversations about the impact of race on education: *counter-storytelling, permanence of racism, Whiteness as property, interest convergence, and the critique of liberalism.*

Counter-Storytelling

Because race influences every experience an individual has in America, one cannot assume that experiences, events, policies, procedures, and practices yield the same results for people who are White as they do for people of color. Counter-storytelling provides different perspectives that help educators acknowledge and appreciate what life is like for students and families whose experiences may be different from their own.

There are, of course, at least two sides to every story. Counter-storytelling is a technique that allows the listener to hear more than one perspective about any event. Think for a moment. What story did you learn about the creation of the countries which currently exist on the continents of North and South America? Chances are your recollections are based on information received from just one perspective—that of the newcomers who changed the face of the existing societies. Every society records events in one way or another and it is very likely that the stories told by historians of the societies that existed centuries before they were "rediscovered" would see the events through a very different lens and tell a different story.

In a perfect world, all ways of thinking, acting, knowing, and being would be accepted and valued based on their ability to solve the social problems of the day. However, "Whiteness" reigns supreme and serves as the standard against which all people are measured. Counter-stories remind us of the danger of assuming there is a single story that can explain any event. They invite us to learn about the life experiences of others that may be very different from our own. Sharing counter-stories provides new knowledge that can lead to changed behavior that could help eliminate race as a predictor of achievement.

Permanence of Racism

The permanence of racism suggests that Whiteness, as a social construct, is the foundation for all political, economic, and social structures (DeCuir and Dixson 2004). Many characterize racism as a deeply rooted and divisive force in American society whose manifestations are commonplace (Sue et al. 2007). Racism is often invisible to those who reap its benefits while it is very visible to those who constantly deal with the realities of inequity.

Racism prevents people not classified as White from accessing rights and privileges that those classified as White take for granted. Examples of the permanence of racism can be seen in the fields of medicine (Ford and Airhihenbuwa 2010; Smedley and Smedley 2005), housing (Smith and Stovall 2008), and appropriate to this discussion, education (Ladson-Billings and Tate 1995; Solórzano and Delgado Bernal 2001; Olsen 1998).

One may say that laws prevent discrimination; however, laws cannot control every action of an individual or the thoughts that lead to an individual's actions. The permanence of racism creates an unequal playing field that leads to disparate results. We must acknowledge this reality if we are to counteract the effects of racism and prevent further occurrences.

An example of the permanence of racism on an institutional scale is the way the federal government directs school districts to measure student success. Federal mandates require school districts to report the results of standardized tests by racial categories. All other student groups are compared with White students as the standard when school districts report disparities in test scores, graduation rates, suspension rates, and other indicators. In a world where the permanence of racism did not exist, groups would not be compared based on race. Racism continues to be a permanent fixture that remains embedded in every facet of American life (DeCuir and Dixson, 2004). If systemic remedies are to be effective, open and honest discussions about the realities of racism are required.

Whiteness as "Property"

For one group to have power and privilege, another group must be in a subordinate role. "Property functions of whiteness include the rights of disposition, the rights of use and enjoyment, reputation and status property and the absolute right to exclude" (Ladson-Billings and Tate 1995).

Within each race, there is a normal variance in intellectual capacity. However, students identified as being in need of special education services are more likely to be Black and Latino than White. Students who are Black and Latino are also more likely to receive special education services in self-contained classes or separate programs. These placements often deny students access to the types of educational challenges that prepare other students for success in society.

On the other end of the spectrum, White students are overrepresented in advanced courses, honors classes, and gifted programs. McIntosh (1988) created a list of unearned privileges that people who are White have come to expect and enjoy even if they did not ask or work for them.

Following the same format, Ruth Anne Olsen (1998) identified privileges that schools confer to students and families who are White. The writer explains that she rarely has to worry about whether decisions constructed at the federal, state, district, or classroom level will reflect an understanding of her children's racial and cultural history. Some of the advantages the author says she can take for granted when reflecting on the schooling experiences of her children are that:

- School personnel will use tests and assessments for making placement decisions for special education or for accelerated programs that are validated using children who share similar backgrounds and experiences.
- Adults in classrooms and in hallways feel positive or have neutral thoughts and feelings about her children's skin color.
- Curricula include worldviews or perspectives that acknowledge her children's racial and cultural history.

- Decision-makers are people who share her children's racial and cultural experiences.
- Role models in print and in media look like her children.
- People in positions of power look like her children.
- Materials are readily available on whatever topics her children choose to explore on the accomplishments and contributions of people who look like them.
- Her children's behaviors, whether positive or negative, are viewed as individual acts and not as acts that support stereotypes for an entire racial or ethnic group.

Identifying the manifestations of White privilege in schools is an essential part of dislodging inequitable practices.

Interest Convergence

Interest convergence is the idea that gains for marginalized groups can occur only when they are of benefit to Whites. Many White Americans say they believe in racial equality, yet few demonstrate the diligence or the collective will that is required to eradicate "racialized" practices that affect educational, social, political, and economic structures. In addition, attempts to address discrimination and inequality meet with resistance from those who believe they may lose advantages or have little to gain from working for equity (Caraballo 2009).

Examples of interest convergence are often the topics of school board meetings and are readily apparent in every school district. For example,

- Magnet schools placed in poor or minority neighborhoods that offer two types of aracdemic programming appear to be for the benefit of the community members; however, closer examination reveals the students who live in the neighborhood are not included in the specialized programming. Their education lacks the accoutrements of the flagship programs while those attending the magnet program receive specialized funding, innovative instruction, and highly trained teachers.
- White parents who challenge the legality of programs designed to prepare students who are Black, Asian, Latino, or first in their families to attend college.

- Administrators who refuse to allow affinity groups that support student development, citing them as exclusionary.

Applying the theory of interest convergence to conversations about the ways personal perceptions influence students' success helps educators to identify the true beneficiaries for policies and programs. This is an essential step in creating equity in schools.

The Critique of Liberalism

The critique of liberalism reminds us that we must be vigilant in dispelling myths that have slowed the process of creating equitable schools. Four ideas that are widely discussed in the literature are notions of *color-blindness, neutrality, incremental change,* and *equality.* Each of these myths contributes to sustaining inequitable practices and maintaining business as usual in schools.

Many adults believe children do not notice differences in the appearance of others or the subtleties in the ways adults treat their peers. The reality is that children begin to recognize race and notice racial differences before the age of three (Tatum 1997). No one enters a learning environment as a race-neutral being.

In the absence of facts, children, similarly to adults, tend to create justifications for questions left unanswered. Once those ideas take root, it is difficult for most to unlearn behaviors or learn new behaviors. Unconscious biases can affect interactions with others throughout a person's lifetime. When we fail to create opportunities for intentional discussions, we perpetuate the status quo rather than becoming agents of change.

Color-blindness does not exist because it is impossible for any social situation to be neutral; therefore, neutrality cannot exist. Teachers and students live "racialized" experiences that influence the ways they interact in a classroom.

More than 50 years since the *Brown v. Board of Education* decision, it is evident that moving with "all deliberate speed" handicaps or further disables the children who are most in need. Segregation in schools and classrooms continues. The concept of *incremental change* contributes more to maintaining the status quo than it does to creating equitable environments for children.

Equality is a moral ideal that invites us to treat everyone the same way. The problem with the idea of equality in education is that once an individual acknowledges that experiences and perceptions lead to different outcomes, it becomes irresponsible to act as if every child begins school on the same footing. "Nothing could be more inequitable than to treat every child equally and then expect him/her to finish with the same level of success" (Singleton 2009).

Racial patterns are not fixed, and remedies do exist. We can no longer allow the marginalization of children based on arbitrary social constructs. When we maintain the status quo, we rob humanity of the opportunity to develop the talent that may address issues and challenges of the day that this generation and previous generations have been unable to solve. The critique of liberalism reminds us of the vigilance that is required to dispel the myths that prevent schools from making the progress in combating racism and the racist practices that are the result.

Discussions around counter-storytelling, permanence of racism, Whiteness as property, interest convergence, and critique of liberalism can uncover long-standing practices and notions that prevent schools from meeting the needs of students in marginalized groups. Naming the behaviors, thoughts, and ideas that lead to current systemic inequities empowers educators to address old problems in new and different ways. Critical Race Theory provides a framework that educators can use to begin to understand the pervasive nature of racism.

Knowledge of CRT is the first step in creating the background knowledge educators need to make systemic change. The second step is becoming aware of the ways personal assumptions, biases, stereotypes, and preconceived ideas influence daily practices. When educators combine knowledge and awareness, and recognize that their behaviors influence their work, constructive differences in educational outcomes for students who represent marginalized groups become achievable.

THE FIRST INGREDIENTS

In 1994, Arlington Public Schools created a process called Futures, a series of meetings in which staff, parents, and community members worked together to create a new vision that would improve the quality of education for all students. Members of the Futures Task Force wanted a superintendent who would design a district-wide plan to address racial disparities. They selected Robert Smith.

Smith maintained that professional development was most effective and most likely to yield changes in classroom practices when teachers designed and conducted their own independent research. He believed staff could create solutions to challenges that lead to gaps in achievement when provided with accurate information about racial patterns and a framework to guide their work. He invited building-level administrators to conduct site-based research focusing on improving the process of schooling. This significant precursor began a shift in the way the district designed professional development.

Shortly after Smith's arrival, a national emphasis on educational standards emerged, forcing educators to acknowledge populations whose lack of success was previously hidden by their White peers' relative success. Even though the district disaggregated data in the past, the new mandate created a level of accountability that was previously lacking. Conversations about the failure of schools to prepare students socially, emotionally, and academically have been persistent in minority communities across the United States. Conversations about the lack of success with minority children now became the focus among APS staff.

Generally, systems do not change without an outside influence. The No Child Left Behind (NCLB) legislation forced the school district to examine the successes of specific populations that were masked by aggregated statistics. The superintendent provided the focus; the federal government provided the mandate and an infusion of funds. These factors contributed to district-wide focus on organizational cultural competence.

In 1997, Arlington Public Schools received a Gaining Early Awareness and Readiness for Undergraduate Programs (GEAR UP) grant. GEAR UP had three goals: to increase the numbers of students who were eligible for postsecondary education; to increase and build capacity among staff and community entities; and to provide parents with information needed to advocate for and support children's academic success.

Because GEAR UP funds could not supplant or replace initiatives that were already in place, the infusion of funding provided opportunities to try new ways to address long-standing challenges. GEAR UP funded workshops to prepare parents to communicate effectively within the home, to support student success in schools, to establish effective communication with staff, and to become involved in the design of policies and procedures that affected students locally. Because of these experiences, a small but powerful group of Black and Latino parents emerged as advocates. The newly empowered parents joined with veteran advocates in addressing the academic needs in their respective communities.

Superintendent Smith created the Superintendent's Advisory Committee on the Elimination of the Achievement Gap that included parents, staff members, and community members. Parents who participated in GEAR UP sessions joined this group. The advisory group identified the challenges students face, reviewed national, state, and local data, and provided recommendations designed to improve racial achievement patterns.

The advisory committee members also participated in the design of the APS Strategic Plan Goals that would guide the work of the district from 2005 though 2011. Subcommittees created the language, timelines, and suggested indicators for each goal. Each subcommittee included the newly empowered parents, members of the advisory group, and representatives from the schools and community.

Words are powerful, and committee members paid careful attention to the language used in the Strategic Plan Goals. Parents and staff wanted the Strategic Plan Goals to identify the elimination of gaps in achievement, to create learning environments that address each child's unique experiences, and to improve communication with the community at large. Members of the Superintendent's Advisory Committee believed that explicitly identifying the elimination of gaps in achievement, as a priority, would be the first step in creating and sustaining an environment where dialogue about the impact of race could occur.

Another conversation focused on whether to use the terms "reduce" or "eliminate" with respect to the goals. Some participants wondered if the use of the word "eliminate" was too lofty given the time period of the strategic plan. Others felt that using the word "reduce" would not create the sense of urgency needed in order to achieve any of the goals. In the end, the Strategic Plan committee created a document that they believed sent a strong message using clear and succinct language. The document provided measurable goals that would eliminate race as a predictor of achievement.

The goals adopted by the School Board in 2005 were:

GOAL 1: RISING ACHIEVEMENT
Ensure rising achievement for all students on standardized tests and other measures of performance that go beyond state and federal standards.

GOAL 2: ELIMINATE THE GAP
Eliminate gaps in achievement among identified groups (Asian, Black, Hispanic, low-income students, students with disabilities, and English language learners).

GOAL 3: RESPONSIVE EDUCATION
Prepare each student to succeed in a diverse, changing world through instruction and other school experiences responsive to each student's talents, interests, and challenges.

GOAL 4: EFFECTIVE RELATIONSHIPS
Build effective relationships with parents and the community so that they know about and actively support the education of our students.

BUILDING CAPACITY THROUGH PROFESSIONAL DEVELOPMENT

GEAR UP funds also provided for professional development. The process began with the revitalization of the Teacher Expectations and Student Achievement Program (TESA). This program is based on the premise that educators' "attitudes, values and beliefs are demonstrated through verbal and nonverbal behaviors through interactions with students, families, colleagues and communities" (Hallam 2009).

TESA uses a combination of research review, self-reflection, and peer observations to increase participants' knowledge of the ways intended and unintended messages transmit through their behavior. The program focuses on skills that improve student/teacher relationships and elevate students' engagement and achievement. TESA research maintains that teachers and other professionals:

- Interact with students based on what they believe they can do.
- Have preconceived ideas about student groups that lead to racial achievement patterns and profoundly affect student success.
- Contribute positively or negatively to student outcomes based on their expectations.

- Demonstrate their expectations through the amount and quality of interactions with students. (Los Angeles County Office of Education 1988)

During the life of the grant, more than 500 teachers participated in TESA. The course began with two trainers.

In addition, GEAR UP provided several new professional development opportunities. The Educator's Quarterly Roundtable discussions allowed participants to talk about current literature focusing on the state of educa-tion for racial and language minority students. Members talked about the marginalization that staff and students feel and the need to move from rhetoric to action.

The professional development that followed focused on the effects of culture on learning. Teaching Across Cultures (TAC), Improving Total Minority Achievement Through Teacher Experience Related Seminars (IT MATTERS), Seeking Educational Equity and Diversity (SEED), and Courageous Conversations for Administrators helped teachers identify and use the cultural assets to enhance learning. Detailed descriptions of the TAC, IT MATTERS, and SEED are included in Tim Cotman's and Marty Swaim's Chapters 6 and 7 respectively.

Each of the courses addresses the needs of the district as well as the needs of individuals who enroll. Every session begins with the same format so participants know the purpose of the session. Professional development includes an enduring understanding and essential questions that clarify the purpose of the work. Group norms and shared defini-tions deepen conversations. An awareness of the systemic nature of the problem is always present, and classes include dialogue about identity, racial identity development, White privilege, and the relationship between power and oppression.

The use of statistics, vignettes, guest speakers, videos, pictures, songs, and poetry keep the voices of children in the room. Rather than dwelling on the societal factors that are out of the control of participants, activi-ties focus on changes in daily interactions with others. Each professional development opportunity incorporates realistic applications in the form of practice so that participants can begin to see themselves as agents of change.

As the professional development menu expands, other needs emerge. The instructors quickly learn that content knowledge alone is not sufficient. Instructors also need skills that help them attend to the emotional needs of participants, and help participants reflect on their professional practice and implement techniques with a renewed sense of purpose.

Professional development for trainers included workshops provided by the National Multi-Cultural Institute (NMCI), the Mid-Atlantic Equity Consortium (MAEC), the National Center for Responsive Education Systems (NCCRESt), and Beyond Diversity and Results-Based Facilitation (RBF). Each of these organizations offers helpful strategies and techniques, and each provides a specific set of skills that complements the tasks.

Originally, trainers believed they were to teach and convince their peers that racism exists, and this caused frustration for all parties. However, the most recent professional development, Results-Based Facilitation, led to a shift in the way trainers view their roles. This slight shift had a huge impact on the quality of interactions with group members. At the end of each professional development activity, presenters ask a series of exit questions that identify the ways the professional development process can improve. The questions are:

- Who needs to participate in this professional development activity?
- What additional information do you need to further your professional growth?
- If given the task of designing this professional development activity, what would you do differently?
- Will you encourage your colleagues to participate in this professional development?
- Would you be interested in being a trainer?
- What have you learned or relearned that will influence your interactions with staff, students, and families?
- What are you still curious about?

Each professional development activity contributed to the design of the next. The use of exit questions led to professional development for district administrators and members of departments that support schools. The course entitled Courageous Conversations for Administrators allows participants to begin to think about the characteristics of a culturally responsive school or workplace. The original intent of the

Table 5.1. Number of Professional Development Participants by Year: 2001–2010

Courses Offered	2001-2002	2002-2003	2003-2004	2004-2005	2005-2006	2006-2007	2007-2008	2008-2009	2009-2010	2010-2011	
Numbers of Participants											
Educator's Round Table Discussions	15	20	—	25	28	15		—	—	—	103
IT MATTERS		12	14	20	22	17	—	—	—	—	85
The Mid-Atlantic Equity Consortium		4	16	16	30	—	—	—	—	—	66
National Multi-Cultural Institute		2	3	10	3	2	2	—	—	—	22
Teaching Across Cultures	10	12	15	15	11	—	1	1	—	—	63
National SEED Training		3	3	3	2	2	1	1	2	—	17
SEED 1		-	8	8	12	18	19	20	20	19	124
SEED 2				11	13	—	—	19	—	15	58
National Center for Responsive Education Systems				—	1	1	2	—	—	—	4
Community SEED				8	12	10	9	8	8	—	55
Administrative SEED					11	18	—	—	—	—	29
Courageous Conversations for Administrators					—	183*	183*	183*	183*	184*	—
Results Based Facilitation						—	—	15	75	48	138
Site Based Cultural Competence Professional Development						—	—	900	900	500	1400
TOTALS	25	53	59	116	145	266	216	246	1188	766	3080

*These numbers reflect the entire administrative staff in the district.

sessions was to prepare administrators to implement workshops with their staffs. However, many administrators indicated that they were not comfortable leading conversations about race and privilege. This led to a change in plans.

While administrators continued to participate in courageous conversations and discussion groups, approximately 108 teachers prepared to facilitate similar conversations in the schools. Armed with the knowledge from a decade of planning, Arlington Public Schools was ready to implement district-wide staff development focusing on the skills, attitudes, and behaviors in order to develop relationships and to work effectively in cross-cultural situations in their schools.

Table 5.1 provides an overview of the professional development that built capacity for a sustained professional development designed to create a culturally competent environment for staff and students in the Arlington Public Schools. The next three chapters will provide details about the specific professional development experiences and the journey of the Council for Cultural Competence in the Arlington Public Schools.

LESSONS LEARNED

Here are several lessons we learned about creating and conducting successful professional development exercises on this sensitive and often difficult set of issues:

Know Your District. It is important to know the culture of your organization, the language, and the ways of doing business. Similarly, no two school districts operate in exactly the same manner. Take the best that your colleagues and allies have to offer, seek new sources of information to add to your work, and do not be afraid to test new ideas.

Listen, Listen, Listen! Stakeholders provide invaluable feedback that will improve the process. You can learn as much from those whose viewpoints differ from yours as you can from those whose views are similar. Listening, really listening to everyone and developing questions of genuine interest, helps others to articulate their point and provides information that will make your product more useful. Using the feedback you receive also validates stakeholders, making them feel that they are an important part of the process, and can achieve the "buy-in" you need to accomplish your goal.

The Only Constant in Working with People Is Change. Therefore, building capacity is essential. Put procedures in place so that newcomers can be included. Archiving essential reading in the professional library can help. Also have a continuous cycle of training and always prepare more people than you think you will need in order to maintain capacity.

Have an Elevator Speech. An elevator speech is a succinct, compelling response of no more that 200 words, to address the recurring questions and related themes. Our elevator speeches address the questions mentioned in Alvin Crawley's chapter (Chapter 8).

There Is a Part for Everyone to Play. Appreciate the work that each person does, no matter how small the contribution or amount of time. Everyone offers skills and perspectives that can be helpful to the process. In any endeavor, there are 20% who will never "come on board." Include them in the conversations but *focus on developing the awareness, skills, abilities, and talents of the other 80%.* Allow each person the dignity to decide what group he or she will join.

Keep Your "Eyes on the Prize." Remember that the goal is to serve children.

Take Care of Each Other and Celebrate Small Successes. Just as there needs to be a safe place for participants to share, facilitators need a venue where they can debrief, reflect, and rejuvenate. Talking about race and working with others to end racial patterns is not easy. However, every child and every one of us deserves our best effort. All of us will be better because of the work.

Share the Joy. Talk with others about your successes as well as your mistakes. This can help them to avoid the same mistakes as well as make sure the road is easier for those who also embark on the journey.

REFERENCES

Bernier, Judith D., and Tonette S. Rocco. 2003. *Working in the Margins of Critical Race Theory and HRD 2003.* Presented at the Midwest Research to Practice Conference in Adult and Continuing, and Community Education. Ohio State University, Columbus.

Caraballo, Limarys. 2009. "Interest Convergence in Intergroup Education and Beyond: Rethinking Agendas in Multicultural Education." *International Journal of Multicultural Education* 11: 1–15.

Coello, Helena, Jorge Casanas, and Tonette Rocco. 2004. *Understanding Critical Race Theory: An Analysis of Cultural Differences in Healthcare Education.* Retrieved from http://www.rt-image.com/1206critical

Conley, Dalton. 1999. *Being Black, Living in the Red: Wealth and Social Policy in America.* Berkeley and Los Angeles: University of California Press.

———. 2001. "A Room with a View or a Room of One's Own? Housing and Social Stratification." *Sociological Forum* 16: 263–280. Retrieved from http://www.jstor.org/stable/685065

DeCuir, Jessica T., and Adrienne Dixson. 2004. "So When It Comes Out, They Aren't That Surprised That It Is There: Using Critical Race Theory as a Tool of Analysis of Race and Racism in Education." *Educational Researcher* 33: 26–30.

Delgado, Richard, and Jean Stefanic. 2000. *Critical Race Theory: The Cutting Edge*, 2nd ed. Philadelphia: Temple University Press.

———. 2001. *Critical Race Theory: An Introduction.* New York: New York University Press.

Douglass, Frederick. 1890. *The Race Problem: Great Speech of Frederick Douglass Excerpted by the National Humanities Center from a Speech Given for the Bethel Literary and Historical Association, Washington, DC.* Retrieved from http://nationalhumanitiescenter.org/pds/maai2/politics/text2/douglass.pdf

Du Bois, W. E. B. 1897. "The Conservation of Races." *The American Negro Academy Occasional Paper*, No. 2.

Feagin, Joe R. 1999. "Excluding Blacks and Others from Housing: The Foundation of White Racism." *Cityscape: A Journal of Policy and Research* 4: 79–91.

Ferguson, Ronald. 2009. "Narrowing the Achievement Gap." Keynote presentation for Administrative Conference for Arlington Public Schools. Arlington, VA.

Ford, Chandra, and Collins Airhihenbuwa. 2010. "Critical Race Theory, Race Equity and Public Health: Toward Antiracism Praxis." *American Journal of Public Health* 100: 30–35. Retrieved from http://ajph.aphapublications.org/cgi/content.abstract/100/S1/S30

Hallam, Maura K. 2009. "Another Piece of the Language Learning Puzzle: Why Teacher Dispositions Are a Crucial Aspect of Student Success." *Language Educator* 1: 26–29. Retrieved from http://www.actfl.org/files/TLE_Jan09_Article.pdf

Hilliard, Asa. 2004. "Ten Conditions for Creating Schools That Work for Black Children." Presented at the Third Annual MSAN Teachers' Conference. Arlington, VA.

Ladson-Billings, Gloria, and William Tate. 1995. "Towards a Critical Race Theory and Education." *Teachers College Record* 97: 40–68.

Los Angeles County Office of Education. 1988. *Teacher Expectations Student Achievement Manual*. Los Angeles, CA: Author.

Massey, Douglass. 2005. "Racial Discrimination in Housing: A Moving Target." *Social Problems* 52: 148–151.

McIntosh, Peggy. 1988. "White Privilege: Unpacking the Invisible Knapsack." Working Paper #189, Wellesley College Center for Research on Women, Wellesley, MA.

———. 2009. "White People Facing Race: The Myths That Keep Racism in Place." Minnesota: Saint Paul Foundation.

Noli, Pamela. 2009. "Addressing the Achievement Gap Through the Lens of Rigor, Cultural Proficiency and Courageous Conversations." Presented at the Courageous Conversations Summit, Baltimore, MD.

Olsen, Ruth Anne. 1998. "White Privilege in Schools." In *Beyond Heroes and Holidays: A Practical Guide to K–12 Anti-Racist, Multicultural Staff Development*, edited by Enid Lee, Deborah Menkart, and Margo Okazawa-Rey, 83–85. Washington, DC: Network of Educators on the Americas.

Pollock, Mica. 2003. "How the Question We May Ask Most about Race in Education Is the Very Question We Most Suppress." *Educational Researcher* 30: 2–12.

Randall, Vernellia. 2002. "Institutional Racism in Health Care." *University of Florida Journal of Law and Public Policy* 1: 45–91.

Romero, Victor. 2003. "Critical Race Theory in Three Acts: Racial Profiling, Affirmative Action and the Diversity Lottery." *Albany Law Review* 66, Part 2: 375–386. Retrieved from: http://www.albanylawreview.org/archives/66/2/CriticalRaceTheoryinThreeActs-RacialProfilingAffirmativeActionandtheDiversityVisaLottery.pdf

Singleton, Glenn. 2009. "Beyond Diversity II." Pre-conference presentation presented at the Courageous Conversations Summit, Baltimore, MD.

Singleton, Glenn, and Curtis Linton. 2006. *A Field Guide for Achieving Equity in Schools: Courageous Conversations about Race*. Thousand Oaks, CA: Corwin.

Smedley, Audrey, and Brian Smedley. 2005. "Race as Biology Is Fiction, Racism as a Social Problem Is Real: Anthropological and Historical Perspective on the Social Construction of Race." *American Psychologist* 60: 19–26. Retrieved from http://www.history.ox.ac.uk/hsmt/courses_reading/undergraduate/authority_of_nature/week_8/smedley.pdf

Smith, Janet, and David Stovall. 2008. "Coming Home to New Homes and New Schools: Critical Race Theory and the New Politics of Containment." *Journal of Education Policy* 23: 135–152.

Solórzano, Daniel, and Dolores Delgado Bernal. 2001. "Examining Transformational Resistance through Critical Race and LatCrit Theory Framework." *Urban Education* 36: 308–346.

Sue, Derald, et al. 2007. "Racial Micro-Aggressions in Everyday Life: Implications for Clinical Practice." *American Psychologist* 62: 271–286. Retrieved from http://www.olc.edu/local_links/socialwork/OnlineLibrary/microaggression%20article.pdf

Tatum, Beverly. 1997. *Why Are All the Black Kids Sitting Together in the Cafeteria? And Other Conversations about Race.* New York: Basic Books.

Thompson, Audrey. 2001. *Summary of Whiteness Theory.* Retrieved from http://www.pauahtun.org/Whiteness-Summary-1.html

Yinger, John. 1998. "Evidence of Discrimination in Consumer Markets." *Journal of Economic Perspectives* 12: 23–40.

Yosso, Tara J. 2005. "Whose Culture Has Capital? A Critical Race Theory Discussion of Community Cultural Wealth." *Race Ethnicity and Education* 8: 69–91.

Chapter Six

Facilitating Conversations about Race

Timothy Cotman Jr.

APS invested in cultural competence training because district leaders believe that changing the attitudes of staff members will transform the system and increase the achievement of students of color. This chapter describes the creation and evolution of Improving Total Minority Achievement Through Teacher Experience-Related Seminars (IT MATTERS), one of the cultural competency seminars offered to APS staff members in the initial development of cultural competence training within the district. The chapter also discusses Seeking Educational Equity and Diversity (SEED) seminars.

The chapter will emphasize the more meaningful activities staff experienced during the seminars as well as evidence of the heightened awareness based on their journal entries. This chapter will also describe my experience as a facilitator of cultural competence initiatives.

A committee of stakeholders that included parents, APS staff members, and community members produced an African American Student Achievement Action Plan in 1994 to address the underachievement of Black students in Arlington County Public Schools. The district placed minority achievement coordinators in middle and high schools where Black students made up at least 25% of the student population. My position as Minority Achievement Coordinator originated from that plan.

The plan focused on collecting data, working with students individually and in groups, and keeping parents of Black students abreast of pertinent information. It wasn't long before my colleagues and I realized the plan was focused on direct contact with the students, but did not address school staff or students' families. It seemed to focus more on "fixing the kids" as opposed to taking a more holistic approach that would empower parents and enhance the skills staff members need to work effectively with a diverse student population.

I began working as Minority Achievement Coordinator in May 1996. Several weeks into the position, members of the district's Office of Minority Achievement were asked to present a workshop that highlighted strategies for working effectively with Black students. My colleagues and I began planning a workshop for one of the high school programs in Arlington. Since I was new to the office, I was given a very minimal role in the workshop; I was to present a handout to staff members that had tips for working effectively with Black students.

At that time my colleagues and I were using the book *From Rage to Hope: Strategies for Reclaiming Black and Hispanic Students*, by Crystal Kuykendall, as a resource as well as resources produced by the Mid-Atlantic Equity Consortium. This particular presentation was to become the "How Not to Do a Workshop" workshop. Cheryl Robinson and I gave it that name because there were factors that, in hindsight, did not create the ideal situation for a presentation.

For example, the workshop was held at the end of the school year. Even if we had done a stellar job, the staff would have had to wait until the following year to implement the strategies. What's more, the staff members did not seem overly enthused to be there; some walked in the room, took one look at us, and walked right back out! Although we thought we had planned well, we were new to presenting and really didn't understand the amount of time and effort it takes to plan an effective workshop. Looking back it has become one of those things where you realize you had to start somewhere.

THE FIRST STEP

Recognizing that there was work to be done beyond direct contact with the students, the Office of Minority Achievement began to create and implement workshops for parents and APS staff members in 1997. Sheila Mingo, the supervisor for the Office of Minority Achievement, charged Minority Achievement Coordinators with creating workshops for teachers. One of the first workshops we offered to teachers was entitled Communicating Effectively with Families.

The workshop highlighted cultural characteristics of a variety of races and ethnicities in order to increase staff members' awareness of how these differences may affect school experiences as well as the perceptions of students and their families. This workshop was well received, and many participants suggested it should be mandatory for all APS staff. We also created a workshop entitled Culturally Affirming Teaching Strategies, which was designed to provide teachers with strategies for developing lessons plans that are relevant to students' lives.

There were a lot of changes to the Office of Minority Achievement during my first years on the job. For example, our positions as Minority Achievement Coordinators, which began as full-time positions in one school, were split into half-time positions between two schools. My full-time position at Thomas Jefferson Middle School became a half-time position and the other half of my position was designated for countywide responsibilities.

When Cheryl Robinson was appointed supervisor, she asked me to serve as an instructor for a course for APS staff entitled Understanding and Relating to Diversity in the Classroom. It was a 10-session seminar through which participants could earn college credit from George Mason University. The course examined how race, class, and gender affect student achievement. The course was actually a compilation of workshops and small group activities we had used in previous years with a few additions.

This was my first time serving as an instructor for a course, and it was a challenging yet rewarding experience. It was challenging because I had always envisioned instructors as experts on the subjects they were teaching, and though I felt knowledgeable about the subject matter, there was still a lot more I needed to learn. It was rewarding because I enjoyed observing educators dialogue about ideas that we rarely discussed.

I went about trying to create an environment in which we could learn from each other, and it worked well. One issue educators shared was that they felt overwhelmed because they worked with such a diverse student population and would not be able to learn every detail about so many different cultures. I explained that the point was not to know everything about a particular culture but to learn about other cultures while creating an environment within the classroom that values and respects differences. I also emphasized that students bring their culture with them and that it was important to create opportunities in the classroom for their culture to be affirmed.

The seminar was organized around small group activities, group discussions, and journal prompts. Each seminar began with a discussion question. At the end of each session, I assigned a journal prompt around an issue we had discussed that day or were going to discuss the following week. Participants also had the choice of writing about anything that we covered that made an impression on them.

The journal assignment after the first session asked participants to define "culture" and describe their culture based on that definition. I believed it was important to define terms we often use and to begin to examine our own culture as a starting point to learning about others. One lesson I stressed throughout the seminar was that learning about others begins with learning about us. Other journal topics included

- What factors contribute to or perpetuate the achievement gap?
- Which factor has a greater impact on the achievement gap: race or class?
- Did African American students receive a better education in public schools before or after integration?

Some of the participants expressed their displeasure with having to write journal entries. Ironically, some of those same participants turned in journal entries that showed great reflection and growth. I was able to learn more about their thinking, and it provided an outlet for participants who did not speak up in class. Throughout the seminar, we emphasized seeking different points of view.

One activity the class participated in early on was the game BARNGA: A Simulation Game on Cultural Clashes (Steinwachs 1990). BARNGA is designed to create conflict by having members play a card game in which there are actually different sets of rules. Everyone believes they are playing by the same rules and they are not allowed to speak as they play, so the conflict escalates. Seeing the dynamics between participants who each have learned to play by a different set of rules is interesting. One participant reflected on her experience in her journal entry:

> Unbeknownst to the rest of us, everyone was playing by different rules trying to teach each other their rules. Some let go of their beliefs of the rules and learned new ones, while others resisted and stuck to their rules. Fortu-

nately, everyone in the class was calm and dealt with the situation without getting too hostile. But the discussion afterwards really opened my eyes to the fact that every time we interact with someone we bring with us our own beliefs or set of rules that are not necessarily the same as others. And in order to communicate we have to be willing to listen and learn the new rules and see how the two rules can be compromised into one set of rules.

We then debriefed the activity by applying the experience to the school environment. We asked, "How does this simulation apply to the school environment?" and "What are some situations where we believe we are all playing by the same rules but in reality we are not?" We focused on interactions between home and school, colleague and colleague, and student and teacher.

One example of playing by different rules was shared by a guest speaker to our class. I invited Patricia Yurrita, Hispanic parent liaison at Thomas Jefferson Middle School, to share strategies for working effectively with Hispanic students. She explained that some parents from Latin American countries are confused by the notion of students who are promoted to the next grade but have not mastered all of the skills at their current grade.

Yurrita shared that this practice is different from practices in Latin America in that students are not promoted if they have not mastered all of the skills at their current level. She also shared that many parents from Latin American countries regard teachers with such high esteem that they may not understand why a parent would have to advocate for his or her child. The teacher would always have the child's best interest at heart and would be the final authority. This is another example of "different rules." In the United States, it is common practice for a parent to advocate for his or her child.

There was a lot of positive feedback from participants in the seminar, and I believe we were able to have discussions that many of them had been interested in having but did not necessarily have a venue for. The participants were able to better hear each other when they were allowed to be vulnerable. At times toward the beginning of the seminar, some participants wanted to be heard more than to listen to others, but toward the end they began to appreciate one another's perspectives. For this reason, I suggested that we change the duration of the next course offering from 10 sessions to 15 sessions.

Understanding and Relating to Diversity in the Classroom evolved into Improving Total Minority Achievement Through Teacher Experience-Related Seminars (IT MATTERS). Both seminars were designed to encourage participants to discuss issues related to diversity and minority achievement and to reflect on their own beliefs and practices.

Libby Romero, an APS staff member, was hired to supplement the lessons from Understanding and Relating to Diversity in the Classroom with other materials to create IT MATTERS. IT MATTERS followed the same structure as Understanding and Relating to Diversity in the Classroom, but we were able to cover more information because we had more time together with the five additional sessions.

IT MATTERS

When people in a group begin to bond, they feel as though they are one entity working toward the same goal. I constantly remind participants that although they are alike in that they have come together to discuss important topics, they do have very different perspectives. Similarly, participants may think they are going to learn about other people and different cultures when in actuality, the foundation for increasing their awareness about others is learning more about themselves and their own culture. Another participant shared this reflection:

> I am at a place in my life where I am in self-discovery mode and the issues covered in this class allow me to look inside myself and examine my belief system. It has been a very interesting process. I didn't always like what I saw when I looked at myself. I believe that my mind is more open and aware now, and that some long-held attitudes have changed. Of course, there is farther I can go, and I will, in time.

IT MATTERS participants took the Implicit Association Test, an online assessment designed by researchers at Harvard to determine if a person is biased against people of a particular group. I assigned this test because it is important to recognize that we all have biases whether we are conscious of them or not. Several types of implicit association tests are available; participants were asked to take at least two tests and one had to focus on race. Participants then wrote about their results and whether they agreed with them.

The session following this assignment was always lively. The first thing some of the participants said on their way into class was that the test was not valid. I explained that I was not as concerned about the results as I was that they focus on the experience of facing their own bias. This process can be difficult and uncomfortable, but it is a necessary step to working with diverse populations.

One participant wrote in her journal:

> During one of our class sessions, we were asked to take an Implicit Bias Test on the internet. I thought the test would tell me some hidden bias that I have had all my life and I felt ashamed at first at the outcome. After our class on bias, I began to not feel ashamed about my personal bias. It is not the fact that you have an initial bias towards someone or something, but it is what you do with the bias thought.

Another goal of the seminar was to allow staff members an opportunity to rethink their views on specific topics. For example, we each have our own idea about what parent involvement means. Some educators conclude that if they do not see parents regularly, those parents don't care about their child's education. One participant wrote in her journal:

> Well, I get it now. In a way I always got it but I have felt that in order for these families to rear successful children they must be able to drop every-thing for a conference or phone call . . . that they must conform to the way we do things, this is America and they must get used to it. I would never say those words aloud but I do think them. Since this class began I have made many changes in my approach with parents and have taken a good long look at my students' home environment. I have tried to build the trust that I have read about.
>
> This class has taught me that successful teaching is as much about at-titudes as it is about methods and techniques. This seminar has helped me to identify some prejudices and preconceived ideas that I have unknow-ingly allowed to impact the way I teach. As I stated somewhat differently in one of my journal entries, being aware of those attitudes and stopping oneself from attending to preconceived notions about a child because he/she belongs to a certain group or performed a certain way on a test battery, and making every effort to attend to the special qualities of each individual student, will go a long way towards helping that child achieve his/her full-est potential.

There are a few experiences I had as a facilitator that I did not fully understand in the moment but after some time was able to understand. One such incident happened during an activity called The Color Line Experiment. The Color Line Experiment was taken from Glenn Singleton's video, *Closing the Achievement Gap: Featuring Glenn Singleton* (Singleton 2002), and it was designed around Peggy McIntosh's article, "White Privilege: Unpacking the Invisible Knapsack" (McIntosh 1989). The activity is found in the implementation guide to the video.

Participants read statements that relate to the individual's perception of the impact of race on his or her experiences and assign each statement a value corresponding to whether the situation was "always," "sometimes," or "seldom" true. When all of the statements have been assigned a value, the participant adds the numbers. The sum gives each person a score, and participants are asked to line up according to their score.

I have participated in or observed this activity at least 10 times, and inevitably the line ends up with the majority of participants of color at one end and the majority of White participants at the other. This particular time was no exception.

However, during this particular exercise, as everyone was lined up, one of the participants, a Latina woman, hurried back to her seat, took a camera out of her purse, and took a picture of her classmates on the line. Then she got right back into line. It wasn't until a few weeks later that I understood why she had taken the picture. She saw the picture as evidence that our experiences or at least our perceptions of our experiences are affected by race. Some people say that race does not matter, but she took that picture as evidence that it does!

CHALLENGES OF FACILITATION

At times I was aware of what was happening with regard to the dynamics in the seminar but I did not know how to respond. Such was the case during an incident that took place around the third session of the seminar. We began the class with a prompt that related to the topic for the day and the class was going smoothly. Participants were sharing ideas and there was a great sense of mutual respect.

As I passed out handouts, I listened to the discussion around the prompt. One of the participants, a White woman I'll call Jennifer, was sharing a story about her experience living in a Southern town. She related a story about a man in her neighborhood who had a pickup truck with a very distinct horn and a Confederate flag prominently displayed on a pole at the back of the truck. He drove around the neighborhood blowing his horn and showing off the flag.

Jennifer did not like the fact that he displayed the flag so prominently because she was against what she felt it stood for. She said she and her neighbors decided one day that they had had enough so they took the flag off his truck. She seemed pleased that she and her neighbors had done this, almost as if she were bragging about their triumph.

A class member, a White woman I will call Lauren, also had grown up in the South and had a very different view of Jennifer's story. Lauren was quiet up to a point and then said, "Well I grew up in the South and you better believe you would not have done that in my neighborhood!"

Lauren explained that she had been raised to take pride in the Confederate flag. After she articulated her feelings, many of her classmates began to question how she could embrace the Confederate flag. They insinuated, not so subtly I might add, that if she did embrace the Confederate flag, she must be racist!

As the discussion escalated, I tried to move participants from the emotional state they were in to a discussion around symbols and how they mean different things to different people, but this was to no avail. I had lost control of the class. Several people were wondering aloud whether Lauren should be working with minority students.

I looked to my left at one point, and saw a Black teacher sitting in the front row silently crying. I will never forget her expression. She wasn't making a sound, but tears were rolling down her face. After a few more comments Lauren grabbed her belongings and ran out of the room. I went after her and caught up to her in the hallway. She said she felt that she was being attacked and that she could not stay in there any longer. Although she had enjoyed the class up to this point, she would not return. She also confided to me that this was not the first time she had been questioned about her beliefs and pride in the Confederate flag.

I told her I was sorry things had gotten out of hand. When I returned to the classroom, it was obvious that everyone was extremely uncomfortable. Jennifer apologized and said she had not meant to offend anyone. With so many things running through my mind I began to think more about the different information we are taught in our schools and at home. For example, Lauren referred to the Civil War as the War of Northern Aggression. I had not heard that before.

As a Black man, I had my own views of the Confederate flag and what it meant. If I had been a participant and not the facilitator, I may have been quick to label her as well. But in this case, I saw a woman who was passionate about teaching, passionate about her Southern heritage, and trying desperately to defend herself against being labeled a racist. As a participant in the seminar, Lauren had often shared teaching strategies she used with her students and her contributions to class discussions were insightful. Now she had left the class and I had to figure out what to do next.

This upheaval took place within the first 15 minutes of class. We still had more than two hours ahead of us. Slowly and cautiously, the class members began to discuss what had occurred, and the strangest thing happened. We had what I would consider the most open and honest discussion to that point.

One Black woman said she did not feel bad for what had happened because as a Black person she felt attacked all the time! The woman I observed crying shared that the conversation brought back memories of when school officials in Prince Edward County, Virginia, decided to close the schools rather than integrate them. Her family members who lived there at that time moved to another state because the schools were closed. Some of them never earned a high school diploma.

As the discussion continued, class members questioned each other and listened in a deeper, more deliberate way. It was a great discussion. But I did not have the skills to guide the class toward that same kind of discussion again without introducing conflict and pain. It shook my confidence as a facilitator because I felt responsible for the conflict. How could I lead discussions that might go places I could not handle?

Lauren came back to class the following week. It took her a while to participate to the same degree as she had, but I was glad she came back. She had sent me a note right after that incident saying that she did not want to continue in the seminar and that it meant a lot to her that I had come after her in the hallway. She had then changed her mind since she did return to class.

I began participating in trainings offered by the National Multi-Cultural Institute (NMCI) and quickly realized how much more effective I would have been had I been trained first! In hindsight, I would have reminded participants that even though we were in the seminar together, we might not agree on the issues.

I would have stopped Jennifer as she was telling her story and asked what she thought someone who took pride in the Confederate flag would have thought about her story. I would have told the class that if something offended them, they should say "Ouch" and then educate the class about why they were offended. Lauren may have said "Ouch" rather than seething as she listened to Jennifer's story.

I wished I could have used this as a teachable moment to discuss symbols and their meanings to different people. But again, I was not skilled enough at the time. I will always remember that experience.

SEED TRAINING

Several years into facilitating IT MATTERS, Marty Swaim, Cheryl Robinson, and I participated in a week-long Seeking Educational Equity and Diversity (SEED) training. I had never before experienced such an intense training. We discussed different types of "-isms" and their impact on society. We shared our own experiences, some of which were very personal and very painful. I left that experience with a much greater awareness of the different ways people are oppressed. I also left with a new focus. I wanted to not only increase participants' awareness but also to motivate them to take action!

Marty, Cheryl, and I facilitated a SEED seminar that first year after being trained and have offered at least one SEED seminar each year since then. Marty and Palma began Community SEED seminars targeted toward parents and community members and we have offered SEED II seminars as well. Each year the school division has sent at least two people to be SEED-trained. The remainder of this chapter will provide reflections in their own words from participants who have participated in SEED seminars offered through the Office of Minority Achievement.

The first reflection is on a particular assignment from a SEED seminar: a cultural exploration. Participants were asked to choose a culture they wanted to learn more about and then participate in an activity that would provide them with greater knowledge of that culture. Most of the participants selected activities related to religion. The following reflection is the response to a cultural exploration:

> As I tried to focus and pay attention and keep an eye on my precocious daughter, I thought about students who come to school not knowing English. How frustrating it must be to go through the day only gleaning bits and pieces of what teachers say. For me, knowing this would be over in an hour allowed me to focus. Our second-language learners come back every day despite not being proficient in English. That is resiliency. I don't know how often I would want to attend mass if I knew I would not be able to understand what was being said.
>
> At the end of mass I ran into a former student who seemed surprised to see me there. She said, "I didn't know you were Catholic!" She thought it was "pretty cool" that I came to the Spanish mass. We chatted a little bit and she introduced me to her mother. Later I reflected on this encounter. What a great way for teacher and student to see each other in a new light.
>
> —Phil Hayden, middle school social studies teacher

Additional reflections are on the overall experience of participating in the seminar.

> People really have to want to end racism and not just talk about it. The elimination of racism would take a people on a heart-searching journey. Some of us are afraid to take that ride . . . afraid to take that ride because at the end of their journey they might discover their true feelings about people who look different from themselves.
>
> —Irene Pleas, middle school special education teacher

> This has been an awareness raising class—awareness of how my own identity was formed as a woman and as a white person. I have also had the opportunity to hear other people's stories and thus have greater insight into ways that we experience life differently based on our cultural perspective and upbringing. The first step toward understanding other people is becoming aware—of both the differences between us and the similarities we share.
>
> —Delores Bushong, high school resource teacher for the gifted

> With the class coming to an end and as I reflect back, I realize that I did not truly examine my own biases as I thought I had. I learned that my biases are

not kept at home and disappear when I come to work. Even though you do not physically react to those thoughts, those thoughts are still in your head. It is very important that you continue to revisit what biases you may have and understand where they stem from. Understand that many of the biases that you have thought of were most likely influenced by others around you and probably from significant individuals from your childhood. To truly help your students overcome racial tensions or conflicts, realize what biases reside in you.

—Veronica Covarrubias, high school guidance counselor

I need to embrace the fact that all my students are different, not the same, and that things such as gender, race, class, and sexual orientation do matter. No, I can't cure the injustices that exist, but I can be open-minded and an active listener and let my students develop their own voice. Certainly, I should use my experience to offer suggestions and actively encourage a child, but I also need to realize that there's a fine line between offering help and providing opportunities versus not valuing the child's own opinions and imposing my values.

I think the most important thing is to actively listen to your students and never to assume you know what they are thinking or what's best for them. Most importantly, care about each student and treat them individually with respect.

—Laura Partridge, middle school math teacher

I have to advocate for my immigrant students because most of their parents do not do so. For many immigrant parents the orientation to the school system is such that they see us as the final authority and they fail to challenge the status quo. The class reminded me to walk with parents on their journey, and be as sensitive as I can to their circumstances and backgrounds.

Being born into a race or socio-economic group of privilege may be nice for the perks it brings with it, but unfortunately the aura of privilege often blinds one person from seeing others with empathy and perspective. This point was made clear in the film, "The Color of Fear." If there is one thing that I hope you will take away from that movie it's the importance of trusting others' perspectives. If someone says they've experienced oppression or bias in their lifetime, dismissing the notion only exacerbates the problem. To have true empathy you must have trust.

When you meet someone at a crossroads be sure to take into consideration the path they have traveled to get to you. If you can keep that thought in your mind you will have the ability to make a difference in your own life and the lives of others.

—Mary Brown, middle school reading teacher

One idea that came up in class that really struck me is the contrast between intent and impact. I firmly believe most teachers have good intentions, but most of us probably don't think as deeply as we need to about impact. To really make a difference in the achievement of our minority students, we need to shift our focus to impact—what is the effect of what we are doing, not how much we want it to work or how much effort we put into it. This is a hard shift—I hear teachers (including myself sometimes) talk about how much work they did, or how much they tried to help a student, and complain about how the student did not respond. If what we are doing is not working, no matter how good our intentions are, we need to change it.

—Shari Benites, high school English
teacher/minority achievement coordinator

LESSONS LEARNED

One of the most important lessons I have learned through the years is that we are each part of the problem and part of the solution. I am part of the problem when I do not reflect on my own biases and the impact they have on my interactions with others. I am part of the solution when I speak up when I observe inequitable policies or practices. The goal is to continually move toward becoming more of the solution and less of the problem.

As I reflected on my experience as a facilitator of seminars on diversity, cultural competence, and racism, I came up with a number of lessons learned along the way. I share them in the hopes that they will prove beneficial to others who are engaged in similar work.

Resist the Idea That You Need to Be an Expert

As a facilitator, remember that you do not have to know everything there is to know about cultural competence, institutional racism, and other issues that will come up in these conversations. Let participants know you will learn from them just as they will learn from each other. You are facilitating discussions but you, too, are on a journey.

Continue to Develop Facilitation Skills

It is not enough to have a passion for the work; you need to have the skills necessary to facilitate. Continue to seek opportunities to strengthen your skills. Just as this work is a journey without an end, your journey to becoming a master facilitator does not have an end. There is always room to grow.

Establish Discussion Guidelines

Discussion guidelines are crucial in creating a safe environment for participants to share and question their beliefs. The facilitator is responsible for creating this environment. Be sure to remind participants of the guidelines often and hold them accountable for adhering to them. You want them to speak from their own experience, refrain from generalizing, and be open to hearing different perspectives.

Trust That Growth Is Occurring

At times you will see growth in awareness happening right before your eyes and at times you will think participants are not growing much at all. Remember that we are each at different points along the journey and even if you don't see growth, ideas have been planted. Resist the urge to judge someone else's journey.

Take Care of Yourself

This is difficult work in that it requires a great amount of reflection and emotional energy for participants as well as facilitators. Be sure to have hobbies, interests, and other outlets that help you to recharge and allow you to focus your energy in other areas.

REFERENCES

McIntosh, Peggy. 1989. "White Privilege: Unpacking the Invisible Knapsack." *Peace and Freedom*, July/August, 10–12.

Project Implicit. "Implicit Association Test." Retrieved from https://implicit .harvard.edu/implicit/

Singleton, Glenn. 2002. *Closing the Achievement Gap: Featuring Glenn Singleton [Manual]. Video Journal of Education* 12(1) 6–7.

Steinwachs, B. 1990. *BARNGA: A Simulation Game on Cultural Clashes [Manual].* Yarmouth, ME: Intercultural Press, Inc.

Chapter Seven

Teaching Across Cultures

Marty Swaim

In the previous chapter Tim Cotman describes the experiences of APS teachers in the IT MATTERS course, for which they earned credit from George Mason University. These teachers began to think about race and culture from a student's point of view and began their own process of self-examination and discovery as adults.

This chapter recounts the classroom and workplace research experiences of teachers, counselors, and assistants in a three-credit graduate George Mason University course I taught for Arlington Public Schools called Teaching Across Cultures: Curriculum and Instructional Strategies for Success With Culturally and Linguistically Diverse Students Developed Through Literature and Conversations with Parents (TAC).

Participants began by developing a knowledge base about the major cultures of their students. They then developed a question of professional interest about their teaching practices with such students: "What if I did . . . ?" This chapter uses their journals and final research essays to demonstrate the changes in their thinking about race and culture that occurred during this class and about the changes they therefore made in their classroom or workplace practice. The chapter provides evidence suggesting that the academic success of some students of color improved as a result of these changes in pedagogy.

THE INITIAL STEPS

My search for appropriate pedagogy to support the success of students of color started in my ninth grade world history class at Arlington's

Wakefield High School in 1984. I discovered that able Black boys, APS students since kindergarten, could not pass essay tests because they could not put in writing the ideas that they could express orally. I asked myself:

- What could I do to teach these students to write?
- How could the best-funded school system in Virginia produce able young Black students who could not write?

To address the first question, I studied with the Northern Virginia Writing Project. Answering the second question continues. I read literature of Blacks, Latinos, and others. I talked with Latina and Black colleagues at Jefferson Middle School where I worked from 1990 to 2001. I worked on pedagogy in my own classroom; Ron Ferguson's five Core Tasks best describe what I did in social studies that helped students of color succeed. However, at this time in my career, I had not read Ferguson's writing.[1]

While serving on the Superintendent's Advisory Committee on the Elimination of the Achievement Gap, I listened as Latino and Black parents struggled to make themselves heard and understood by the primarily White staff and committee members. It seemed to me the participants were often talking past each other because the same words meant different things to each of them. The staff did not understand the world of Latino and Black parents. If the staff knew more about these parents and their children, I thought, they could communicate better with parents and their students. Better understanding might lead to better student success.

So in 2000, I drafted a course outline for teachers using some of the same writing I had used in my world history classes, chosen from the classical literature of these cultures. These works included *The Souls of Black Folk* by W. E. B. Du Bois, *The Bluest Eye* by Toni Morrison, *The Death of Artemio Cruz* by Carlos Fuentes, *Woman Warrior* by Maxine Hong Kingston, and others.[2]

I began with the goal of helping participants develop a basic knowledge of what it meant to be Black, Latino, and Asian, what life was like for the children they taught who were non-White, and what kinds of experiences parents and students of those cultures had in the Arlington Public Schools. Race was a natural part of the conversation.

The premise of the class was that educators' knowledge of student culture was the foundation for building relationships with students and for demonstrating respect, thus increasing the chances of student success. The premise is sound: building trust and interest is the first of Ron Ferguson's five core tasks in producing successful students of color.[3]

At the beginning of the course, race was a part of but not the focus of the curriculum; the primary focus was on understanding other cultures. I learned about and gained an understanding of race and racial identity development along with the class participants—my teacher colleagues.

My first class included one Montessori teacher, Marlena Dasbach, of German and Filipina parentage, who knew from experience about racial identity development and Whiteness. She had taken a SEED class (such as we began to teach in 2003) in a private Montessori school in Massachusetts. Marlena brought me Peggy McIntosh's article "Unpacking the White Knapsack," a beginning discussion on White privilege and racism, and told me about Beverly Daniel Tatum's book, *Why Are All of the Black Kids Sitting Together in the Cafeteria?*, which articulates, among other things, how racial identity develops in all of us. These readings became a part of the course, as did *Dreamkeepers: Successful Teachers of African American Children*, by Gloria Ladson-Billings. It discusses the characteristics of the teachers of students of color who succeed.

In 2003, I expanded the focus of the course from knowing other cultures and conversations about race, to include Whiteness (an understanding of ourselves), and pedagogy.

The focus of the course expanded to race and Whiteness because we were reading material on Whiteness and listening to real-time stories about how parents and students were affected by race. The staff in these classes were generally quite open to the study of Whiteness, and willing to consider the relevance of White privilege in teaching students of color.

The parents who told their stories to the classes were not generally hard on the school system, but they all had stories to tell about judgments made about them or their children based on race: the Black female doctor whose offers to come for Career Day were ignored, but whose services were always solicited when the school needed food for an event; the Black mother who received the free-lunch form four times until she called the school secretary and explained that she did not qualify for free lunch; the dark-skinned Latina whose children were inappropriately placed in special education; and the Black mom whose son was refused enrollment in an advanced math class even though he met the prerequisites.

Parents also shared stories of discrimination in their own lives—stories that most of the White participants found eye opening and disturbing. The participants of color shook their heads knowingly, and often shared their stories. Thus the course began with the goal of learning about others, and came around to a concurrent goal of knowing about ourselves as White people, Black people, Latinas—all people with a race.

DISCOVERY ABOUT RACE, WHITENESS, AND RACIAL IDENTITY DEVELOPMENT

At the end of the semester, participants were asked to choose their favorite passages from the semester's readings and explain why they chose that particular passage. What follows are teacher writings in response to that assignment. The writers are native English-speaking White women teaching in majority-minority schools, except where noted.

The writing shows real change in the teachers' knowledge of themselves as White people, including the importance of affect in teaching, the areas of their personal knowledge that need work, and their understanding of the complex consequences of racism for people of color and for themselves as White people. These are subtle changes in teacher knowledge that are important for connecting with students and their families.

A third grade teacher in a majority White school wrote the following about a passage from *The Bluest Eye* by Toni Morrison:

"Here [in the white household's employment] she [Pauline] found beauty, order, cleanliness, and praise. . . . The creditors and service people who humiliated her when she went to them on her own behalf respected her when she spoke for the Fishers. Power, praise and luxury were hers in this household" p. 128 [Pauline, African American housekeeper, mother of Pecola, who dreams of blue eyes; Fishers, White, her employers].

My reaction: This passage conveyed the power and respect that Pauline had when she was the Fishers' housekeeper. Something she had never experienced before. It was probably one of the happiest times of her life. The fact that she neglected her family was so sad. "They became afterthoughts one had just before going to sleep." This passage really made me think about the lack of identity that Pauline felt and how she tried to cope. The culture of minority students needs to be valued. They should never

feel that they are an afterthought or not equal to a White student. Sandra
Franzen, 2/07/06

A speech therapist in a majority White middle school chose these passages from *The Souls of Black Folk* by W. E. B. Du Bois. She wrote:

> "A double life, with double thoughts, double duties, and double social
> classes must give rise to double words and double ideas." *The Souls of
> Black Folk*, W. E. B. Du Bois.
>
>   It seems to me that one of the greatest advantages to being in the major-
> ity . . . is not to have to worry about double anything. This reminded me
> of Wise's contention that white people benefit from racism—and made me
> think of all that I've taken for granted [Tim Wise, *White Like Me*].
>
>   [Reaction] "Racism lies at the center, not at the periphery; in the perma-
> nent, not the fleeting." This was a thought provoking statement. It made me
> picture racism as a material "thing" that had shape and mass and weight,
> instead of as an ethereal, flitting phenomenon that is hard to grasp. This
> gave me a sense (I think) of the unrelentingness of racism—or its poten-
> tial—for those who have or might experience it . . . made me think about
> racism in a more "affective" way, instead of in the more cognitive way I
> had approached it before.
>
>   You cannot connect what you are teaching to students' lives and their
> histories if you do not know what they are. It logically follows that you
> need to know something about African American experience in order to
> fully and effectively exploit the teaching approaches/strategies Ladson-
> Billings describes. This is where I am decidedly lacking. [The reference is
> to *Dreamkeepers*, by Ladson-Billings.] (Melissa Stone, 2/12/07)

A middle school English teacher wrote,

> The words of W. E. B. Du Bois opened a window into the world of the
> African American that I did not understand. I came to empathize with what
> it must be like to enter a room as a black and know that each person in the
> room, white or black, is thinking about the color of the skin. "It is a peculiar
> sensation, this double consciousness, this sense of always looking at oneself
> through the eyes of others, of measuring one's soul by the tape of the world
> that looks on in amused contempt and pity." (Nancy Tiernan, 2/07)

These teachers show change in one of the most important aspects of behavior in building a successful classroom for all students: knowing who

they are themselves. Their responses show honesty about race that is basic to building relationships of trust and interest and thus starting students on the complex road to success.

TEACHER RESEARCH

In the mid-semester assessment of the second year of the course, three teachers asked to apply their newfound consciousness about Black and Latino identity development to their teaching by actually trying different pedagogy. I agreed, and by the 2002–2003 school year, reflection on classroom or workplace research was a part of the course.

The formal mid-course assignment for teacher research was preceded by brainstorming on possible research questions using prompts such as "What would happen if I did . . . ?" "What do I want to fix, start, or change?" One session included a discussion of qualitative research and data collection.[4]

The formal assignment asked participants to do an informal study of what works in the workplace or classroom to improve the school success of Black and Latino and Asian students.[5] They were to select a characteristic/behavior/event they had not tried before that they thought was one possible key to building the success of students of color. This could be teacher behaviors and expectations, and related pedagogy such as patterns of questioning, books and materials, physical classroom arrangements and classroom management, skill development, relationship building, lessons directed to a specific need, parent and community related activities.

Participants would keep a running journal about their research, record rough data and keep relevant material, and develop a 750- to 950-word essay describing their research and the results, keeping in mind that the question they were researching might not be the one they got answers for.

RESULTS OF TEACHERS' RESEARCH

The teachers engaged in TAC teacher research described their changed knowledge, behavior, and practice in relationship to students of color and issues of race—their own race and that of their students. These teachers took to heart the discussions on the pedagogy needed to support students of color and tried new practices that by their accounts increased the success of their minority students. These efforts required new behaviors on the part of the teachers—and new behaviors mean hard work.[6]

Teacher research papers submitted by 31 of the 46 TAC teachers over five years show self-reported changes in important teacher behaviors related to student success, and many of those teachers collected data about specific academic successes among Black and Latino students.[7]

The subjects of their research fall into six important areas of pedagogy:

- Three researchers did work that began with *self-examination*: "What have I been missing or avoiding in how I work with students and their parents?"
- Six implemented and evaluated an *intervention* with respect to a struggling student; the result of the intervention was a new relationship and a solution.
- Seven used *student culture* to connect to required academic material.
- Four used *student strengths* to increase participation and success.
- Three focused on *communication*, setting out to increase minority parents' participation.
- Eight tried different ways to push minority students to excellence, what Ron Ferguson calls *developing ambitiousness and industriousness.*

The following selections reflect each of these major areas of pedagogy.

Self-Examination: What Have I Been Missing or Avoiding?

Selection 1

The research subject here is how to increase minority participation in Individual Education Plan meetings. The method included interviews conducted by a middle school special education teacher with Black and Latina colleagues about IEP meeting practices and revisions in practice to reflect that advice.

What Have I Learned? . . . I have a better understanding of why parents walk into my room [for an Individual Education Plan meeting] the way they do. My African American parents have reason to feel frustrated with schools, and to be angry if their child is not successful. . . . Educators carry with them the aura of White privilege. I needed to understand the hurdle my being White (however worthwhile my intentions) can be for minority parents. I needed to be reminded of the hundred, if not thousands of subtle or overt racial slights these parents have experienced. No wonder their guard is up.

Regarding the Hispanic parents I see, I needed to learn how the institution of school itself is threatening, especially with a police officer in the hallways. I needed to be reminded of the experiences of government corruption, deadly police forces, and recurrent disappearances some of them no doubt faced in their countries. (Becky Moore, 4/07)

Selection 2

A middle school guidance counselor wrote:

In taking a hard look at my practice throughout this course, it is evident that I tend to spend more time with female adolescents as they are more outspoken about addressing their social needs.

Journal 17 asked us to define ourselves according to our roles, personality, and appearance and then to describe a student in the same terms whom we feel is a challenge to work with. I immediately wrote about an African American seventh grader, James [not his name]. James is large, stocky, quiet, sullen, angry, reticent, unmotivated and sarcastic, in many ways my opposite. Though intelligent and capable, he is failing classes and appears completely disinterested in his education.

This exercise was an awakening as it was evident that though this student is clearly in need of help, the difficulty in working with someone so unlike me had translated into my focusing attention onto children I viewed as more accessible. Having been touched by the power of adults who make a difference in a child's life, through Nate McCall's stories in *Makes Me Wanna Holler*, to the case studies in *Dreamkeepers* and even the African American parent's reflections, I thought it would be beneficial to reach out and establish bonds with students with whom I have not established rapport.

To reach such a boy, this counselor and the substance abuse prevention counselor formed an anger management group for Black and Latino males. To attend, the boys needed passes from their homeroom. After only a handful of sessions, the boys were conscientious about picking up passes, upset when the group was canceled because of a late opening, and open to sharing and participating. They began to self-refer to counselors for problem solving—a new behavior. In an individual session with the abuse counselor, James was "asked if he trusted M—— (the counselor), he replied that he did." The counselor writes: "This validated that with a little extra effort, I was able to reach a student that I previously found to be my greatest challenge." (Erin Culligan, 2/12/07)

Selection 3

A high school English teacher who is a person of color reconsidered race in the 12th grade literature curriculum for a class of predominately White students:

> I was teaching the Renaissance period to my 12th grade English Literature class. I chose to study Shakespeare's *Othello*, as one of the themes that dealt with racism, which I have skimmed over in past lectures and discussions (about Othello). Students read Peggy McIntosh, "Unpacking the White Knapsack" and the first chapter of Tim Wise's *White Like Me*. This class was . . . [also] reading articles and books about blacks in America.

The research data were collected from questionnaires examining student understanding of racism in the Renaissance and today.

> Students got the idea that "Othello's Achilles heel was his lack of confidence in being a Black man in a White man's world." The Renaissance period was of "rebirth" but not for the Moor, no matter how brave or intelligent. (Millie Solomon, 2/07)

Focus on One Child: Building a New Relationship

Six teachers described what happens if the teacher or counselor focuses on a single struggling student and that child's difficulties. All six research papers recorded the evolution of a new interconnected personal and pedagogical relationship with a child at risk. Five recorded improvements in the area of targeted student behavior, and one had an inconclusive result in that behavior. Two examples follow.

Selection 1

A first grade teacher focused on a Latina child who "arrives late, is inconsistent with homework completion, has many absences, and has a difficult time returning forms and materials. The parents . . . do not appear to be comfortable in the school." (The White teacher is a fluent Spanish speaker in a 90% White school.)

The teacher saw the girl as a child "at risk." The teacher began her efforts to connect with the student by offering an after-school homework club. This offer got no response from the father at after-school pickup, but the teacher persisted and set up a conference. To her surprise, the child's mother came. The mother explained that the child did her homework, the family did respond to notes, and found materials in her bag the next day. What was happening? The child handed in nothing.

When the child was called in, her mother and the teacher discussed these conflicting experiences with her. After tears and reassurances, the child, her mother, and the teacher worked out a plan for a Friday homework lunch, if needed. In fact the improved communication between the family and the teacher resulted in all homework being turned in, and improved attendance and tardiness rates. The teacher and student had lunch anyway, "for the pleasure of each other's company."

This first grade teacher writes:

> Reflecting on my research, I have come to several realizations. First of all, I should not have made my assumptions about the parents not supporting school behaviors, which I did. . . . I should have persevered earlier in the year in trying to connect with the parents. . . . I am aware of the importance of finding someone in the family to connect with in a positive way. [Even if the first contact—in this case with the father—gets no response] . . . I realize the power that having communication has upon the student. [Until we met] the child was in control of both of us. Once we were a united front, the balance of power shifted. (Lisa Morse, 2/1/05)

Selection 2

A third grade HILT teacher (High Intensity Language Training for Students for Whom English is a Second Language) decided to find out what happens when I devote one or more days a week to have lunch with individual students and organize the "reading club" in the morning before school starts. I hoped I would be able to motivate them to complete homework in a timely manner, they would become more receptive to what I teach, the quality of their work would improve and consequently they would become better readers.

(Background: The teacher is a White fluent English speaker, but not native born. Her students are Latino and Black second-language speakers whom she sees 90 minutes a day.)

The teacher began with a lunch for all of her students, at which she and the children shared family pictures. She then had lunch with individual students, in alphabetical order. The morning reading club became popular for a short time. The two students with the worst homework record in the group settled into coming every morning before school to work on their homework while the teacher set up the class.

The teacher writes:

It is my belief that this new student feeling of obligation (to do homework) came directly from the lunchtime meetings and morning reading times together. . . . As we connected they saw my classroom as a pleasant and truly inviting place. My students got to know me and developed a trust that I am here to devote my time and ultimately to help them when they needed help. I also got to know my students. Consequently my students made considerable progress in reading as evidenced in DRP (Degrees of Reading Power) testing. Two of my students who never completed homework started doing their homework. (Beata Chambers, 2/5/04)

In each case, the interventions that focused on a particular difficulty led to a relationship that became important to the teacher and the child. The interventions were so productive for the individual children about whom the teachers were concerned that what began as research on what might help minority children succeed became a part of the teachers' practice.

Using Student Knowledge and Culture in the Curriculum

Seven teachers developed research questions about what would happen when they used the culture and life experiences of their students to teach material. The teachers who wrote new curricula for their classes using these student-connected materials found that their students had greater academic success and were more engaged. Classroom management issues diminished.

Selection 1

A high school physics teacher, a White male in a majority-minority school, hoping to increase student interest in science wrote:

> Will students achieve higher grades on a research paper if the subject of the paper is tied to the student's heritage? [The VA Standards of Learning PH. 4 is] "exploration of the roles and contributions of science and technology." I always thought this was an important SOL because if the students are interested in what science can do, they tend to achieve the other SOLs. This question entails three separate but important strategies to encourage student engagement. The first is project-based learning. . . the second is choice . . . the third is recognition by the teacher that the student's culture is important.
>
> The students were asked to write a 4-page biography about a scientist who might not be on a curriculum list but who is from their home country or connected to their family's history/culture somehow. They could choose anyone they wanted and I suggested that they discuss their choice with their parents.
>
> Compared to the first quarter's project (a research paper), students had higher grades. According to interviews with students, the students found that they were very engaged with their parents and that does not happen very often. Overall they thought the assignment was very good. (Dan Harris, 2/07)

Selection 2

An elementary school teacher asked:

> What will happen if the 3rd, 4th and 5th grade beginning LEP (Limited English Proficiency) students learn the 3rd grade SOL geography terms by making a geography booklet about their countries, applying the terms of their own countries? Will the children learn the terms (in English) along with an opportunity to display pride in their country and culture?

(Background: the class is second language learners primarily from Latin and Asian countries, whom the teacher sees for a part of the day. Students have not always succeeded in this SOL.)

The teacher taught the terms using student journals, maps, the library's picture file, and the terms themselves as spellings words. Students then used the terms in making a booklet about their own country for which they illustrated each of the SOL required terms. Using the common terms and the illustrations from their books, these children who may have no common language were able to talk simply to each other about their country.

> All of the children performed well on the final written test . . . I was surprised by how enthused the children were about the entire project and how easily they mastered the geography terms. Students did connect more with the subject using their life experience. Student scores improved. (Charlotte Georgerian, 1/29/05)

Using Student Assets to Build Student Success

Students bring to the classroom real experiences and skills that may not fit with some teacher needs in classroom organization. The expectation that students will participate in discussions may not match a student's personal situation or learning style. The requirement that a more fluent student sit quietly while others' homework is checked may not fit middle school energy or the fluent student's skill level.

Four teachers looked at these differences that students bring as if they were assets and sought to use them toward the learning goals of their classes. The examples are from high school and middle school.

Selection 1

In an English as a Second Language parenting class for teenage mothers and mothers-to-be, the teacher asked: "What happens when I incorporate dialogue journals into my ESL/Parenting class?" The teacher was frustrated with the lack of participation and discussion. She knew students had stories to tell and were greatly in need of practice in conversation to improve their English. (Background: In dialogue journals, the teacher responds in writing to the biweekly writing done by students. The journal becomes like an ongoing letter.)

I can't believe how much the dialogue journals have changed both my students and the class. It has been one of the most helpful tools that I have ever implemented into my curriculum. I can . . . elaborate on specific topics that were addressed in class . . . it is student driven . . . [A student who is] hesitant to ask, they write it in their journal. . . . One of the most important outcomes of the journal is it has helped me to forge a closer relationship with my students. (Kristin Growitz-Bermudez, 2/1/05)

Selection 2

A middle school teacher who found her class for fluent Spanish speakers contentious and unruly while she checked homework asked, "What happens when the students are divided into groups of 3 or 4, and each group has a (student) leader to practice the dialogues in Spanish?" (an idea from a case study in *Dreamkeepers*).

This teacher, Latina herself, found that by using the superior skills of some of the native speakers to lead a group to practice dialogues as well as coach and check the work of their classmates, she was able to build a class in which the contentious students became the leaders and modeled correct Spanish. Her task of checking work and practicing dialogues was shared, and therefore doable. Students got more language practice than was the case when she checked all papers.

Based on surveys and interviews, the students liked the small groups for language practice, and although the record keeping was work for them, the student leaders liked the challenge. The teacher believed she could provide practice and be "listening to everybody in a more comfortable manner" (Ana Rosa B. Koski-Karell, 2/12/07).

Improving School/Home Communication Across Cultures

Two special education teachers prepared new communication methods before and during Individual Education Plan meetings. Both observed that the lack of participation by minority parents in Individual Education Plan meetings—their often defeated physical appearance, their total lack of questions—was not good for the process or for their child and their child's success in school. Another teacher changed her communication with Spanish-speaking parents about school, homework, and the curriculum more generally. Excerpts from the research summaries of the two special education teachers follow.

Selection 1

An eighth grade special education teacher observed

> African American parents sometimes come in wary, their body language large, leaning into the table. Hispanic parents frequently enter my room with trepidation. Their anxiety shows in downcast eyes, and reluctance to say a word, even if their English skills are good. They sit leaning back in silence . . . grateful for anything positive I say, but seem to sink within themselves when their child's disability is discussed.

This teacher's research interviews with a Latina colleague produced this advice:

> Slow down! Spend time asking parents how they are, is everyone well. . . . It is considered rude . . . to begin a meeting without small talk. . . . Share as well; speak of your own family. Allow time. To tightly schedule meetings with Latino families is self-defeating.

The African American colleague gave some of the same advice and agreed that "the presence of White privilege could be a barrier between my African American parents and me." She suggested: "Always begin with the positive. Invite the parent to talk about their child. Listen for as long as it takes." Be prepared with questions to use with parents who are reluctant to talk, to get them started.

This teacher transformed her Individual Education Plan meeting as follows:

- Hold meetings in the early morning or after school, when time constraints are less.
- Welcome parents at the door.
- Have the Individual Education Plan papers, but do not start with them. Offer food. Start with small talk.
- Speak positively about the student, and then ask questions that will give permission to the parents to talk about their child. (Becky Moore, 4/07)

Selection 2

A middle school special education teacher, after interviews with translators and parents, added a preparation step to her Individual Education Plan meetings with parents. Her interviews revealed that language proficiency and the education level of parents needed to be taken into account in some very specific ways. Having a translator present was not enough to help parents understand the process and the issues for their child.

> Before the meeting I printed up the Individual Education Plan and went over it with my student so that he could go over part of it with his parents. For the meeting I made an outline with simple statements breaking down the meeting into 3 sections:
>
>   1. What do we know about the student? (performance)
>   2. What does the student need? (goals)
>   3. What can the school do to help? (services and accommodations)
>
> My thoughts were written in simple English and (in the meeting) I made sure to stop every 2 minutes or after each transition and ask the parents "Tienes preguntas?" encouraging them to ask questions. I make a point to ask them questions (about their child) to open dialogue.

For the IEP meetings in which the teacher used these changes, parents asked more questions.

> In the future my goals are to find out the level of English proficiency and educational knowledge of the parents prior to the meeting involving the whole team, have a pre-meeting with the translator and parent to go over the findings and prepare parent questions. . . . Create a chart that explains least restrictive environment so that parents know what the team is recommending. Bring common work samples to compare/contrast with their own child's. (Kelly Miller, 2/12/07)

Succeeding at a Hard Task: Building Industriousness and Resilience

Ron Ferguson argues that the tasks of building trust, interest, and student autonomy through conscious relationship building, intervention, and using student culture and strengths are the background for the hard work of moving students to become individuals who internalize a working standard of excellence. The idea is that students internalize that standard for themselves as they succeed at a difficult task, and then another, and so on. Helping students do this is culturally competent pedagogy. Eight teachers took on this challenge. Here is a middle school teacher's account of her efforts.

Selection 1

The research question was about how writing about art might improve the quality of word use, depth, and complexity in the writing of students of color. A sixth grade middle school English literature teacher asked students to write about Who I Am:

> How does art help students improve their writing? How does it clarify the main idea and details? Does the use of sensory words and figurative language increase? Does it help in story mapping, visualizing, describing, explaining? Are students more confident in their writing, more motivated?
>
> Studying the painting: we wrote down what we SAW. Then we interpreted those tools into what we THINK and FEEL. This involves inferencing. We asked questions about the painting, the meaning and unanswered questions. Next we used the vocabulary of the elements and analyzed what we observed about the painting. . . . This process led to descriptive and graphic writing and then to poems that each student wrote and shared.
>
> The next step was Maya Angelou's poem "I Love the Look of Words." Then art work, and the poems written with them in mind, then the process of responding to an art work with your own poem. The final poem that students wrote in this activity was "A Praise Poem" with similes and metaphors using their heritage, skin color, size, personality animals, something in nature, to explain who they are. . . . Integrating another art form, drama tableaus and the use of the thesaurus to find better ways to express their thoughts and feelings helped create more powerful poems. The level of their vocabulary increased, as did the quantity and quality of descriptive words, sensory words, and personal feelings and reactions.
>
> Some of the poetry knocked my socks off! One, . . . the poet is an African American boy, very disengaged from school, with many serious aggression problems. He was so engaged in this activity. He chose an abstract painting called *Melancholia* by Raymond Jonson. His poem resonated with true feelings of loneliness and depression. He is extremely proud of this poem, as am I. As a result of this positive experience he has made a great effort in this class. He was suspended the last week of the term, so he could not finish all of his work. He came in on Teacher Work Day and worked for 6

hours in my classroom. He ended with a B in English, but more importantly with a feeling of pride in the accomplishment for hard work. I can't help but attribute this, in part, to his creative endeavor. (Nancy Tiernan, 2/12/07)

In fact, the six different areas of research chosen by the participants in Teaching Across Cultures roughly match up with the descriptors of culturally relevant teaching written by Gloria Ladson-Billings in *Dreamkeepers* and by Ron Ferguson in the Tripod Project. The self-reported experiences of these teachers show reflection about their practice, change in their behaviors, and frequent improvement in student results.

Furthermore, in 2008–2009, about one-quarter of the teachers who had taken TAC volunteered to take the year-long training to become trainers for other teachers on race, race and the achievement gap, and the practices of culturally relevant teachers. This demonstrates a broad professional commitment among these teachers to removing the power of predictive factors such as race for student success in the Arlington Public Schools.

LESSONS LEARNED

I learned four big lessons from Teaching Across Cultures and my work in training for cultural competence since 2005:

1. White people need to talk to each other about race.
2. In training for cultural competence, use volunteers to start the conversation about race and the achievement gap.
3. Use teachers to train teachers.
4. Build training experiences around stories, the stories of real people.

White People Need to Talk to Each Other about Race

White people who want to see the achievement gap disappear need to talk to other White people about race, racial identity development, and the connection between race and the achievement gap. The idea that Black is bad, incompetent, less, is an idea that some White people created, owned, and drummed into our common consciousness during the past two or three centuries. White culture's success is reflected in CNN News Anchor

Anderson Cooper's interview research project in 2009–2010 in which children of all colors consistently picked White dolls over Black.

Black children in our schools face this perception of "Blackness as bad" every day, among peers, and from the media, although their parents work hard to counter it. White people need to talk to other White people about race in order to

• Understand race and be able to talk about it.
• Remove this pervasive negative perception about race.

Talking about race, breaking down stereotypes, and building communication skills and knowledge among diverse people builds a sound racial identity for our Black children and our White children.

I write this lesson learned as number one because in seven years of teaching the course Teaching Across Cultures and four years of facilitating cultural competence training, I have rarely met a White participant who understood when we started training that

• Race is the condition of life that a child of color meets every morning in experiences that tell him he is not as good as the next kid, and the fact that these experiences are provided by White people who usually do not intend harm, does not make the experience less of a downer for a child of color.
• Racism is the systemic privileging of one group over another, not simply acts of personal meanness. Racism lies in the institutions in which we participate, such as schools, banks, and political parties.

The only exceptions to my experience that White professionals are clueless about race have been White people married to or in committed relationships with a person of color. Furthermore, as our training has expanded to include teachers and other staff who are required to participate as contrasted to the training of volunteers, I have heard a small but significant number of White staff state that race itself is not a relevant consideration in the achievement gap, because "I worked hard and I made it."

Let me share an example of what I think of as simple "not knowing." I participated in a small group discussion in cultural competency training with White teachers in which the question on the table was "What do you think is the connection between race and the achievement gap?" This discussion was early in training on the system's strategic goal of reducing the achievement gap. The intention of the discussion was simply to get out on the table the views of the participants on this question. Everyone starts this training with a variety of assumptions. The assumptions become a benchmark for change.

We paired and shared first. Most people are more willing to talk about race in the larger group if they can talk one-to-one first. A teacher asked me what the question meant. I repeated the question, "How does race affect the achievement gap?" The teacher first said "I do not know," then thought for a moment, and said "Well I guess race means that students of color who come here are more likely to come from one-parent families, be low income, have less preparation."

When the group volunteered their observations, nobody in the room suggested that the simple fact of race, of experiencing negative messages in Arlington, in this school and school system as a Black or Latino child, race itself, might cause children to be less successful. Most participants focused on socioeconomic variables that are associated with race.

Of course economic variables are decisive for some children. On the other hand, research demonstrates difficulties for students of color simply because of race: stereotype threat, racial microaggressions, and other experiences. But in my experience, we White staff do not know how race can affect our students of color. Or how race knowledge absorbed from surroundings influences our White students in their perceptions of color, no matter how non-racist their family.

I am convinced that, in fact, race itself, and the way a child of color is seen by peers, teachers, and the world, profoundly challenges the child's self-image as a competent, ambitious, industrious, achieving child, to use Ron Ferguson's formulation. I am convinced by the stories of my colleagues, parents, and students of color, and by a great deal of published research. For me, this means that schools and teachers need to go out of their way to provide a counterweight to negative perceptions of race through positive achievements and experiences for students of color.

Therefore part of my job in diversity training is simply "'outing" race for White staff by making race and Whiteness subjects we openly discuss. In an early training session such as the one I described, the job of the training is to get all views on the table, not for me to talk about Whiteness. But gradually, many participants discover for themselves the experiences of race that their students of color have, and their own experiences with being White. They also begin to think about what race means for their own personal growth as teachers and what race means for the education of White students.

As a White person I can now see that as a child I did not have to think about race, nor did my children. Our being White was a benefit to us that we could ignore. White was normal. My consciousness of my Whiteness had to be discovered.

In defense of the White staff whose discussion I recounted here, I took 30 years to get to an understanding of my Whiteness, and my privilege, and of the real daily life of Black people. Even though I served on a majority Black, District of Columbia Board of Education, taught at Jefferson with two Black colleagues and a Latina colleague with whom I talked almost every day, read voraciously in the literature of African Americans, Latinos, Asians, Indians, and Middle Easterners, I did not recognize White as a race.

But in 2001 when I read Beverly Tatum, as well as Peggy McIntosh's "Unpacking the White Backpack," I saw that this matter of race was not solely about Black people. From Tatum and McIntosh and others I learned that I have an identity and privilege as a White person, whether I want it or not, because of the history of this country. This was my moment of "knowing differently." In Teaching Across Cultures that moment of knowing differently was reflected in the change of the course from studying others to studying others and examining our White selves.

For White people, talking about race includes rough spots. Tatum has a great discussion about race in her first chapter, and how and why this discussion about race is hard for White people. The chapter bears reading and rereading in order to sort through all that is involved in "outing" race for White people. First, as one training participant explained to me, she was raised to teach as if race was not important because in fact underneath the skin we are all the same. To learn that for her students of color, color matters and is an important part of their identity, was a challenge to her old teaching philosophy.

For some White people, whiteness does not feel like privilege because they got the short end of the White stick: came up poor, not always knowing where the next meal was coming from, worked to put themselves through school. Such White people want schools to pay attention to poverty and its curses before race. They often want to think that anyone can make it out of poverty if they just work harder. Some teachers have this kind of White experience, and their hard times must be listened to in training so they can be open to the fact that the Black or Brown child in their class has an additional kind of hard time to deal with.

Finally, I am constantly struck by how far away many caring and conscientious White people are from knowing that White is a race as much as Black is a race (not biologically but socially), and that White people lead a racialized existence. Helping White people and the people of color among us know each other's true stories of privilege and of hardship is part of what our cultural competency training does.

Start with Volunteers to Initiate
the Conversation about Race and the Achievement Gap

The teachers who signed up for graduate courses such as IT MATTERS, Teaching Across Cultures, and SEED from 1999 to date are the backbone of the trainers who volunteered to be trained as cultural competency facilitators for other teachers in our training program for staff in volunteering schools begun in 2008. These volunteers provide a high level of thoughtfulness and knowledge of the issues in the training because of their experiences talking about race and achievement over time. Using volunteers first builds capacity and quality.

Use Teachers to Train Teachers

The teachers, assistants, counselors, social workers, and other school staff who took our graduate classes and then took training to teach teachers about cultural competence all bring to the task knowledge and commitment. They want the achievement gap gone from their schools, and they spend energy figuring out how to accomplish this goal. Their presence as facilitators in the training provides credibility and skills. This is a model that works in settings such as The National Writing Project, and it meets the standards developed by the National Association of Professional Development.

Build Training Experiences around Stories of Real People

Assessments of the course Teaching Across Cultures always rated very high the experiences of listening to African American, Latino, and Asian parents tell their personal stories, and the stories of their children's experiences in the Arlington Public Schools. Stories connect people.

NOTES

1. Ron Ferguson, Tripod Project, Harvard University. See also The Education Alliance for Teaching Diverse Students, Culturally Competent Instruction; NCREST; James Banks.

2. Course readings for Teaching Across Cultures, GMU, M. Swaim, 2007. Required* books and readings in order of their use in the class:

*Nathan McCall, 1994, *Makes Me Wanna Holler* (416 pages, not all required, Vintage).

*W. E. B. Du Bois, 1903, *The Souls of Black Folk* (278 pages, $2.95, Dover edition). We read about two-thirds of the essays in this book.

*Gloria Ladson-Billings, 1994, *The Dream Keepers: Successful Teachers of African American Children* (127 pages, $17).

*Selections from Beverly Daniel Tatum, Ph.D., 1997, *Why Are All the Black Kids Sitting Together in the Cafeteria?*

*Selections from Toni Morrison, 1970, *The Bluest Eye.*

Selections from Ira Berlin, 1998, *Many Thousands Gone.*

*Rigoberta Menchu, 1983, *I, Rigoberta* (Guatemala; 10 of 20 chapters, 150 pages, $18), **or**

*Carlos Fuentes, 1962, *The Death of Artemio Cruz* (Mexico; 307 pages, $14).

*Mario Bencastro, 1998, *Odyssey to the North* (El Salvador; 192 pages, $12.95).

Mario Vargas Llosa, 1996, Essay: "Country of 1000 Faces," *Making Waves* (Peru; 15 pages).

Mario Vargas Llosa, 1993, *Death in the Andes* (pp. 1–79, $14).

*Gabriel Garcia Marquez, 1984, *A Tale for Children—The Old Man Who Fell from the Sky* (Colombia).

Esmeralda Santiago, 1993, *When I Was Puerto Rican, How to Eat a Guava.*

Juan Gonzalez, 2000, *Harvest of Empire, A History of Latinos in America* (part 1, 58 pages).

*Maxine Hong Kingston, *Woman Warrior* ("No Name Woman," "Shaman," "A Song for a Barbarian Reed Pipe"; 209 pages).

Kien Nguyen, 2001, *The Unwanted: A Memoir* (343 pages, great true story, not required).

3. Ron Ferguson, The Tripod Projects, Five Core Tasks and Stages of Classroom Social and Intellectual Engagement. "Progress is neither smooth nor irreversible. Early stages are often revisited."

Tasks: Trust and Interest vs. Mistrust and Disinterest
   Balanced vs. Imbalanced; Teacher Control and Student Autonomy
   Ambitiousness vs. Ambivalence
   Industriousness vs. Disengagement and Discouragement
   Consolidation vs. Irresolution and Disconnection

Ferguson writes that in order to build trust, teachers must answer these basic questions that Ferguson's research on student perceptions shows students have. "Who are you? Will you like me, and students such as me?" "Are you Fair?" Building trust, in his view, is a combination of information that a teacher provides, their honesty and affect, and their ability to develop relationships built on knowledge of the student and mutual respect. Ferguson argues that when a teacher successfully accomplishes this first task, building trust and interest, he or she is more likely to be able to manage the second, balancing teacher control and student autonomy. Students who feel a relationship of trust are more likely to be willing to work hard, exercise self-control, be ambitious and industrious, that is to keep working when the work gets hard.

4. This material comes from Marian Mohr's writings on teacher research, *Teacher Researchers at Work*, by Marian S. MacLean and Marian M. Mohr, National Writing Project, 1999, and also from materials written by Marian Mohr for a teacher research course in APS.

5. We have few White or light-skinned second language students from Central or Latin American, or from the rest of the world. Therefore our second language students, immigrant or native born, deal with race and its effects on them as do our Black students, in addition to the consequences of learning English as a second language.

6. The reader should note that teacher research projects commonly follow a new practice over six to eight months of the school year. These papers were written after two months of a trial, December–January, although most participants continued the practice that they began in December. Two months of research may provide different evidence than does six months.

7. TAC teacher research participants included K–12 teachers, assistants, librarians, counselors, and a speech and an occupational therapist, all native English-speaking White women, except where noted. Over the five years during which this research was a course requirement, 46 educators participated for whom papers are available. A very small number of papers were incomplete, or not available.

Chapter Eight

System-Level Buy-In: A Case Study

Alvin L. Crawley

Arlington Public Schools is committed to developing a "culturally competent" workforce to assure that staff has the expertise, compassion, and skills to effectively educate all of its students.

Our schools educate some groups better than others, and for too long in American education, race has been a predictor of academic achievement. Simply stated, White students have done better than Black and Latino students. For our society to achieve its highest aspirations, and for our country to succeed in a globally competitive environment, we must eliminate this gap.

To do this, we must make fundamental changes in the way we teach and the way we treat one another in our schools. Our commitment to eliminating gaps in academic achievement requires us to develop and implement policies, practices, and procedures that create a safe, supportive, and equitable learning environment for each child.

In previous chapters, Palma Strand, Cheryl Robinson, Tim Cotman, and Marty Swaim described much of the professional development effort that supported this work in Arlington Public Schools. In this chapter, we describe APS efforts to develop and sustain organizational "cultural competence" as one means to confront the achievement gap. We do this through an examination of the development of the Council for Cultural Competence.

A key lesson we learned from the inception of the "cultural competence" initiative is that building organizational cultural competence requires everyone to be vigilant and steadfast. Any work that requires staff to focus on self and their individual and collective institutional behaviors that support or undermine student achievement has the potential for failure. Engaging staff in the development of organizational cultural competence is a journey characterized by introspection and self-examination on a personal and professional level.

In our experience building organizational cultural competence involved sharing personal stories, some of which were painful; engaging in self-reflection and discovery; disaggregating student achievement data; applying instructional best practices, including demonstrable culturally responsive teaching behaviors; and committing to facilitating high-quality learning experiences for all students. None of this is easy.

Topics related to race and education are often viewed as too controversial, risky, and emotional to confront head-on. However, we know from a historical perspective and review of national data on the academic achievement of Black, Latino, and White students that race continues to be a predictor of student achievement. These findings are prevalent in urban and suburban school districts, with school district wealth less of a determinant of student success for minority achievement than other variables such as access to rigorous courses and positive relationships with teachers or other staff.

The research of Ferguson (2007) and others revealed that the development of effective relationships between teachers and students and their families can make a significantly positive difference in achievement outcomes. According to Ferguson, "there is growing evidence that students are most motivated when teachers are strong on all three legs of the instructional tripod: content knowledge, pedagogic skills, and relationship skills." In a 2008 opening keynote presentation, Gloria Ladson-Billings, noted educator and author, told Arlington Public Schools staff that the two most important skills of any teacher are an in-depth knowledge of subject matter and cultural understanding of students.

Research findings and personal experience suggest that a long-term initiative is not sustainable without an infrastructure that supports it. It supports the policies and practices that provide the opportunity for all students to achieve at high levels.

Implementation of culturally competent policies and procedures is complex practically, politically, and programmatically (Rutledge 2001). Great and worthy ideas die a quick death without the critical support of stakeholders at all levels of an organization, the willingness to confront findings that expose academic inequities in student access to quality learning experiences, and the courage to address findings in an honest and forthright manner.

In retrospect, like many organizations, Arlington Public Schools had a history of offering its staff a variety of diversity workshops. Some diversity-related training activities were integrated into instructionally based workshops. The impetus for a few workshops came about as a direct result of diversity issues that occurred between staff within schools. Initially, these sessions took the form of conflict resolution activities that were specifically designed to clarify or heal misunderstandings that had arisen between individuals or groups.

As we began our current cultural competence efforts, we recognized that while the previous diversity training workshops were well intentioned, there had not been a comprehensive and sustainable plan to engage all staff. In short, there was no infrastructure in which to do the complex work required to achieve the mission.

There was also a lack of clarity as to how this work supported the school board's existing strategic plan that focused on raising student achievement overall and eliminating gaps in achievement between racial groups. Council for Cultural Competence members who had participated in past diversity training inside and outside the school district expressed uncertainty about how our new initiative would be received by district staff and the community.

BUILDING AN INFRASTRUCTURE—COUNCIL FOR CULTURAL COMPETENCE

In our effort to build an infrastructure to support organizational cultural competence, APS staff recognized that there needed to be a permanent "governing body" that met at least three criteria:

1. The group needed to be representative of all levels of the school system. This meant selecting staff from the various employee groups including administrators, teachers, instructional support staff, maintenance staff, and finance staff.
2. The group needed to reflect the racial, linguistic, and cultural diversity of the school district, with attention also paid to gender.

3. Given the voluntary nature of the group, members would be selected,
   or in some cases recruited, because of their training or their personal
   experiences or desire to see changes made in the system.

All participants had an equal voice, so our process had the benefit of all
their varied experiences and perspectives. There was an air of excitement
about the group's potential to have a major impact on staff relationships
and delivery of instruction to all of our students.

The journey toward establishing a permanent governing body to support organizational cultural competence began in 2003 when a group of
13 Arlington Public Schools staff members formed the Diversity Council.
We quickly developed a meeting schedule and ground rules for engagement. Most significantly, we began the process of developing a core set
of values.

The first core value was that, given Arlington Public Schools' diverse
workforce, building organizational cultural competence was essential for
strengthening relationships among staff. The second value was that organizational cultural competence was critical for the successful instruction
of all students—closing the achievement gap—and preparing them to live
and work in a diverse and rapidly changing world.

The group embarked with a sense of urgency and proceeded to make
several mistakes. We did not spend enough time investigating relevant
research. Initially, we should have done a needs analysis of strengths and
weaknesses related to organizational cultural competence, but we did not
do this until later in the process. Similarly, we should have made an explicit link between our work and the school district's strategic plan. The
group also lacked clarity on the individual and collective responsibility of
each council member for sustaining and growing the work.

On the other hand, the lack of a defined road map combined with our
willingness to confront the potential political fallout from exploring the
sensitive topic of race and its impact on schooling set the stage for the
school district to take bold new steps in the form of "courageous conversations"—frank discussions about race and other "sensitive" subjects.
This term was adopted from Glenn Singleton and Curtis Linton's book
*Courageous Conversations about Race: A Field Guide for Achieving
Equity in Schools* (2006). In retrospect, our initial actions inadvertently
support the premise that on the journey to achieving cultural compe-

tence, sometimes you do not know what you do not know! And, it's okay.

Later the same year, several members of the council attended a three-day training session on cultural competence sponsored by the National Multi–Cultural Institute, a District of Columbia–based organization with a national focus on diversity training. The conference exceeded staff's expectations and proved to be a beacon that guided the group through its early development as a council.

After the first day of training, which focused on building a case for organizational cultural competence, several things became clear.

First, the council needed to spend time building a case for why its work was important in the school system, particularly how the work supported the school board's strategic plan goals.

Second, given the financial expenditures and staff time this initiative would entail, the council needed both formal approval and long-term articulated commitment from the superintendent and the school board.

Third, there needed to be a formal mechanism to assess the strengths and challenges of the school system in order to develop a plan that effectively addressed the school system's needs. In essence, this meant an action plan could not be based simply on anecdotal experiences. Instead, we needed a formal cultural audit that engaged representative sections of employee groups. We needed additional documentation and data, including system-wide student achievement data disaggregated by race and program, to provide a rationale for this initiative.

With a renewed sense of purpose, focus, and background knowledge, the Diversity Council changed its name to the Council for Cultural Competence. The council recognized that its professional development initiative would be far greater than the traditional diversity-related workshops staff had been accustomed to attending.

The council identified four specific goals: create a school climate where fairness and respect are encouraged and modeled so everyone enjoys equitable opportunities for professional and personal fulfillment; provide and support programs that explore the experiences, perspectives, and contributions of various cultures, groups, and individuals; implement policies and programs that address diversity related topics and concerns; and provide sustained professional development on diversity-related topics. Most important, the council's work had the potential to serve as a key vehicle in closing gaps in achievement between student groups while supporting the rising achievement of all students.

Given these goals, the district could not view cultural competence activities as an add-on to existing initiatives. Cultural competence activities needed to be viewed and embraced as an essential and integral part of the Arlington Public School's organization, with the mission, goals, and activities woven into the fabric of existing district and school-based operations.

To this end, Council for Cultural Competence agendas focused on activities that ranged from providing members with opportunities for personal growth and development to implementing system-wide professional development activities such as planning Summer Cultural Competence Institutes; organizing the Superintendent's Administrative Conference; producing training and informational videos; writing scholarly articles on cultural competence for district and county newsletters; advising the superintendent on matters related to organizational cultural competence; and planning system-wide training over a three-year period. The council members also spent time developing definitions that would guide their work, recognizing that definitions create a common language and promote mutual understanding for users.

There have been many challenges to ensure we maintain our momentum and there certainly have been and will be bumps in the road, but it is important to accept that engaging in cultural competence activities is not easy work. Resilience and perseverance are keys to sustaining the work. There remains much uncharted territory, in part because there is a paucity of research on the direct impact of cultural competence training and impact on student achievement in public schools. To date, most research has been done in the area of health care systems.

One critical indicator of a successful initiative is its integration into the everyday culture of an organization. While the long-term impact of the Council for Cultural Competence has yet to be determined, some key indicators suggest success.

The 13 members have increased to 31, with an additional wait-list of interested participants. The council produced a cultural competence video featuring students, the superintendent, and members of his leadership team. Furthermore, the council sponsored two superintendent's conferences featuring prominent keynote speakers and providing effective and practical workshops. Workshop topics included: culturally responsive teaching behaviors, Latino/Latina identity, and diversity in the workplace and handling difficult conversations.

SYSTEM-WIDE CULTURAL COMPETENCE TRAINING—SCHOOL BOARD

School board members honored their commitment to the initiative by participating in their own "courageous conversations" group and providing resources in the budget. An independent consultant who had conducted training in the school district teamed with a retired employee who was an active member of the cultural competence initiative to facilitate training with school board members.

At the executive level of the organization, there has been ongoing professional development and public acknowledgment of the importance of cultural competence and its connection to student achievement. Presentations have been made to the public through school board meetings, National Education Association (NEA) Executive Board members, a northern Virginia regional superintendent's group, and the Washington Area Boards of Education, a group comprised of school board members from surrounding school districts. Cultural competence goals are aligned with the school board's strategic plan for goals related to rising achievement, achievement gap, responsive education, and effective relationships.

SYSTEM-WIDE CULTURAL COMPETENCE TRAINING—ADMINISTRATORS

One of the important conversations about building capacity took place in 2006. Members of the Council for Cultural Competence discussed the need to provide central office and school-based administrators with a detailed orientation to their work prior to involving teachers and support staff. This proved to be one of the most strategic moves undertaken by the council with support from the superintendent and school board.

Superintendent Rob Smith required all administrators to participate in large group cultural competence training. Additionally, all administrators were assigned to diverse groups of 12. These groups met on a monthly basis using an APS Cultural Competence Curriculum for Administrators, developed in part by council members, and also work completed through a Virginia Department of Education Cultural Competence Initiative. Administrators reviewed research articles, watched videos, read the book *Courageous Conversations about Race* by Glenn Singleton and Curtis Linton (2006), and discussed student achievement data. These collective experiences were, for the most part, well received by administrators.

In spring 2008, the council sponsored an event featuring a keynote speaker who stirred up a great deal of controversy by citing alleged acts of racism committed by mainstream media and corporations in their portrayal and treatment of Black people in America. Feelings from participants ranged from ambivalence to anger. This two-hour presentation caused some to question the need for the cultural competence initiative, and whether the work would bring staff closer together or increase divisions.

Remaining focused on the larger goal of improving student achievement through organizational cultural competence tested the resiliency of the school district. It also challenged the group to adhere to one of the agreements for courageous conversations: to experience discomfort. Conversely, another renowned speaker electrified and inspired staff with her connection of cultural competence to student learning. We appreciated the presentation and it solidified our belief that any sustainable initiative cannot rely on one presenter, article, book, video, or model.

Clearly, too narrow a focus would doom the work to another promising, but failed diversity initiative. For the next two years, the council continued to provide opportunities for one-to-one, small-group, and large-group discussions and study through articles, reviews of student achievement and personnel hiring data, and feedback on related topics.

Embedded in these actions was the message that we will not always agree on written materials or spoken views related to cultural competence, but we have to consider different perspectives and we have to continue our work. The Administrators' Cultural Competence groups continue to meet through a mixture of 11 small-group meetings and 3 large-group meetings held regularly during the year.

SYSTEM-WIDE CULTURAL
COMPETENCE TRAINING—FACILITATORS

In the summer of 2008, the first group of 21 facilitators went through a four-day Summer Institute on Cultural Competence. The group was a healthy mix of instructional and noninstructional personnel who had expressed an interest in being trained to lead cultural competence training for school staff in the fall. Many of the participants led "courageous conversations" sessions in administrative work groups that had met during the course of the school year.

Participants received training in developing facilitation skills; handling difficult conversations; cultural proficiency models based on the work of Mason; and Stinson's Diversity Awareness Profile. Participants were given opportunities to work in teams to develop and present various modules. The power of personal stories and experiences served as the cornerstone of the training experience.

Building on the momentum from the four-day summer training experience, and in keeping with the contents of the five-year action plan, the council developed and offered a year-long train-the-trainers model, which began in September 2008. The goal of this training was to prepare school-based facilitators to provide cultural competence professional development in schools and departments during the next three years.

Prior to the facilitator training, the plan and proposed implementation timelines were shared with all district administrators for feedback and buy-in. The school board supported the effort through its budget allocation. With the essential support of principals, approximately 108 staff representing all schools and alternative programs were selected to participate in monthly cultural competence facilitator's training.

The council did not establish specific staff selection criteria for principals. Instead, the council advised principals that potential school-level facilitators should have a strong interest in personal and organizational cultural competence; a demonstrated ability to work with diverse groups; a willingness to attend all planned training sessions; and a commitment to remain in the school district during the implementation year.

The curriculum consisted of readings, activities, and programs that we adapted to ensure it met our district's needs. An orientation session was held for interested facilitators to provide an understanding of the relevance of this work to the school system's strategic plan goals, and an opportunity for us to assess their availability to attend required sessions and complete outside preparation activities.

Cultural competence training took place over nine sessions, each lasting two hours. Topics included the racial achievement gap, racial consciousness and racial unconsciousness, interracial dialogue, considering multiple perspectives, White privilege, antiracist leadership, and cultural proficiency models.

The sessions followed a structured format of lecture, group discussion, two- to three-minute paired sharing conversations, and experiential activities to reinforce concepts. Participants met as a large group for the first hour, and then broke into smaller groups of 10 to 12 for the second hour.

Each training session was facilitated by one to three experienced facilitators and started with a review of session objectives, guidelines for dialogue, and communication agreements (see Table 8.1). The small-group sessions afforded participants an opportunity to have "courageous conversations" in a safe environment; ask questions; practice skills learned in the large group; and develop closer relationships with participants from other schools within their group.

We required consistent attendance at the sessions as a condition of participation, in addition to outside reading assignments and school-level activities. The expectation set for participants was that at the conclusion of training, which included participation in a three-day Summer Institute, all newly trained facilitators would have the basic skills necessary to lead cultural competence faculty development in selected schools during the next three years.

Our plan was that each year, beginning in 2009–2010, staff at 13 different school sites would undergo year-long training. Each month, 108 staff trainees worked with their school administrative team to integrate future school-level training into their respective schools' management plan. School and department administrators attended four mandatory training sessions in small workgroups as an extension of their past training.

In January 2009, administrators were asked if they were interested in having their school be in the first tier of schools to undergo training. Those who volunteered worked with representatives from the council to design their own professional development schedules. At the same time,

Table 8.1. Facilitator's Training Modules: September 2008–September 2009 Timeline

Activities	References	Timeline & Duration
Orientation Meeting		September 17th 2 hours (3:30–5:30)
Cultural Competence Framework Cultural Competence Definitions Cultural Audit – Findings and Recommendations Cultural Proficiency Continuum Courageous Conversations Racial Achievement Gap – Critical Factors – Strategies of Cultural Competence Selected Readings Activity 1	APS Plan – Chapter I & II Manual Manual page 12 Cultural Audit Document Page 15 – Manual Singleton, Chapter 2, pg. 13–24 Manual Singleton, page 2	October 15th November 12th 2 hours – 2 hours
Establishing Common Language Four Agreements of Courageous Conversations & Communication Agreements Racial Consciousness and Racial Unconsciousness Discussion of Articles Activity 2	Singleton, Chapter 3 Singleton, page 58 Singleton, page 54	December 10th 2 hours
Race Defined White Privilege Selected Readings and Discussions Activities Activity 3	McIntosh article, Singleton pg. 181–208, Chapter 10 McIntosh White Privilege Tim Wise – White Like Me Chapter 3 Manual	January 14th 2 hours
Considering Multiple Perspectives Interracial Dialogue Creating Safety Activity 4	APS Singleton, page 119, Chapter 8 APS Chapter IV Manual	February 15th 2 hours

(continued)

Table 8.1.   Facilitator's Training Modules: September 2008–September 2009 Timeline
(*continued*)

Activities	References	Timeline & Duration
Anti-Racist Leadership & Closing the Achievement Gap Selected Readings Activity 5	Singleton, page 213, Chapter 11 IEL Article Chapter IV Manual	March 18th 2 hours
Culturally Responsive Standards & Instructional Best Practices Selected Articles Activity 6	Chapter V Manual Singleton, Chapter 12	April 22nd – May 20th 2 hours – 2 hours
Group Development of Facilitation Skills Professional Development Best Practices Planning Organize all materials – Team Planning Time Activity 7	Tips for Facilitators APS Office of Professional Development Use of Data	August – TBD 2 days
All Facilitators will conduct an orientation to Courageous Conversations with their assigned faculties		September – TBD 1 hour

*Activity 1, 2, 3, 4, 5, 6, & 7 will be used during faculty Courageous Conversations.
Note: Second week in September there will be an orientation meeting required for all facilitators selected to participate in the training. This will provide facilitators and the council with an opportunity to address selection concerns and provide participants with an overview of the initiative.

the facilitators in training were asked their preference as to whether they would like to facilitate in their own school or another school.

In assigning facilitation teams, consideration was also given to the location of schools, schedules for staff development, and proximity of the site to the facilitator's work site. The number of facilitators on each team varied depending on the size of the school faculty.

We solicited feedback from the facilitators on the program as training neared completion. Participants indicated they were comfortable with the content but concerned about their ability to facilitate difficult conversations. In response to these concerns, a three-day summer institute was specially designed to give facilitators more skill development and practice in facilitating groups. Training also included team-building activities. An optional fourth day was provided for facilitators interested in learning additional strategies for facilitating dialogue.

SYSTEM-WIDE CULTURAL COMPETENCE TRAINING—SCHOOL LEVEL

In the fall of 2009, Arlington Public Schools was poised to provide professional development for 900 teachers across 12 schools or alternative programs. This represented a third of school district teaching staff. The first session was referred to as the Cultural Competence Kickoff Session. It was designed to bring all school faculties together to hear the same message.

The superintendent set the stage by explaining why this work was important, and its connection to the school district's strategic plan and vision for professional development. Other presenters discussed key terms used in cultural competence, an overview of the training format, and the curriculum. At the conclusion of the kickoff session, one Black senior staff member shared his personal story about growing up in the South and attending an affluent, predominantly White boarding school. The presentation was moving and garnered him a standing ovation. The speaker emphasized to the group the importance of developing relationships with students, having high expectations for student performance, and the need to be advocates of all students. The speaker's story also emphasized the power of stories and the impact that sharing our experiences can have on others.

The training required each school to commit to a minimum of 15 hours of their annual staff development time. Participants received recertification points toward licensure renewal. Hourly staff members received payment for professional development not held during their contract hours. Every participant received a training manual. Participating schools received a set of books that was used as supplemental material. A Blackboard site was developed that housed the manual, additional readings, and articles on audio tape.

Facilitators received lesson plans for each session that could be adapted to meet the needs of staff. To ensure everyone appreciated the relevance of the materials, general system-wide data were shared along with each school's student-level data for comparison purposes.

Despite all of our efforts during the orientation and kick-off session, certain questions still emerged:

1. Why are we doing this?
2. How is this going to make a difference?
3. Isn't poverty the problem?
4. When are we going to get strategies for working with the students?
5. What's next after year one?
6. Why are we using these definitions of race and racism?

During facilitator debriefing, the same questions came up repeatedly, and we tried to understand why. We concluded:

1. Conversations about race and student achievement bring about a range of emotions.
2. These discussions rarely take place in school settings and, because of the discomfort associated with the topic, it is imperative to address these questions as a part of professional development.
3. This work also deviates from traditional diversity training because it focuses on teacher behavior and not student attributes. Thus, these questions were not inappropriate, rather they speak to the point that people are not used to seeing themselves as part of the problem.

The Council for Cultural Competence has been the forum for these activities, in addition to others that have been central to building organizational cultural competence. It serves as a bridge connecting the various initiatives aimed at addressing student achievement and staff's preparation to educate a diverse student body. It also serves as a clearinghouse for ideas that promote cultural understanding and practices that lead to organizational cultural competence.

There is no fairy tale ending, for this work is still in its infancy stage. The Council for Cultural Competence members routinely reflect on and assess strategies to determine which have been effective, ineffective, or have the potential to contribute to sustaining this initiative.

A question the council has revisited is what key variables allowed Arlington Public Schools to sustain the cultural competence initiative, given that many school districts have encountered strong opposition and have been unable to sustain similar efforts. One important variable may be the willingness of the Arlington Public Schools leaders to ask hard questions and openly acknowledge that we have an achievement gap; that is to say, that while overall district student performance was above state and national averages, a significant number of minority students were not making the same gains as their white peers, and that race was a strong predictor of success in the school district.

In response, there was an agreement to engage various school and department staffs in long-term professional development that focused on instructional practice and on examination of behaviors that we determined support or undermine the achievement of minority students. Senior leadership including school board members, senior staff, and principals were given opportunities to engage in professional development aimed at increasing their cultural competence skills.

It has become clear at the highest level of the organization that to eliminate the achievement gap we must have aspirational goals and clearly defined indicators. Small steps can lead to big accomplishments.

CUSTOMER SATISFACTION SURVEY AND CULTURAL COMPETENCE

One strong indicator of whether the school district is viewed favorably in its academic mission are the results of the district-wide Community Satisfaction Survey (CSS) administered biannually. The Community Satisfaction Survey is comprised of 17 questions for parents, 17 questions for community members, and 27 questions for students. Many survey questions have multiple parts. Together they offer a lens into the general satisfaction of the Arlington community of parents, students, teachers, and community members with the public school system.

In 2007, the Council for Cultural Competence worked with staff in the Office of Planning and Evaluation to develop specific questions on the 2009 Community Satisfaction Survey related to student perceptions of Arlington Public Schools as a culturally competent organization. The survey addressed the following perceptions:

- My race and culture accepted by staff.
- My race and culture accepted by students.

- I am comfortable working with students of other races.
- I see pictures/videos/assignments that relate to different cultures.
- I learn about other cultures.
- Teachers treat minority students with courtesy and respect.
- Staffers help students who do not speak English well.
- Staffers react if they observe name-calling or teasing related to race or culture.

The Community Satisfaction Survey findings (see Tables 8.2 and 8.3) indicated that the majority of students responded positively to questions related to staff acceptance of students from different races, visibility of information and pictures with individuals from various racial and cultural groups, treatment, respectful behaviors, learning about different cultural groups, and staff intervention when students hear inappropriate comments.

The latter item had the lowest positive response rate, suggesting the need to provide greater school-wide and district focus on anti-bullying and harassment initiatives. Given that these questions had not been asked in previous surveys, results were considered good baseline measures on which to assess future progress.

We commonly refer to cultural competence work as a personal and collective journey. As the culture of the organization shifts, there is an in-

Table 8.2. Student Responses to Cultural Competence Items on the 2009 Community Satisfaction Survey of the Arlington Public Schools

Item	Percentage Response*			
	Strongly Agree	Somewhat Agree	Somewhat Disagree	Strongly Disagree
My race & culture accepted by staff	62	21	5	2
My race & culture accepted by students	50	30	5	3
Comfortable working with students of other races	77	17	1	1
I see pictures, videos, or assignments that relate to different cultures	39	33	6	4
I learn about other cultures	42	33	6	3
Teachers treat minority students with courtesy & respect	57	24	3	2
Staffers help students who don't speak English well	50	27	4	2
Staffers react if they observe name-calling or teasing related to race or culture	46	26	7	4

Table 8.3.   Student Responses to Items Related to Cultural Sensitivity and Closing the
Achievement Gap on the 2009 Community Satisfaction Survey of the Arlington Public Schools

Response	"I feel students of my race or culture are accepted by staff at school."	"I feel students of my race or culture are accepted by students at school."
	Student (N=998)	Student (N=999)
	Percentage Response	
Strongly agree	61	49
Somewhat agree	21	30
Neither agree nor disagree	9	13
Somewhat disagree	5	5
Strongly disagree	2	3

2009 Results
- To further delve into perceptions on race at Arlington Public Schools, students were asked two additional questions on acceptance within the schools.
- More than four-fifths (82%) of students either "strongly" or "somewhat" agreed that "students of their race or culture were accepted by staff at school"; and 79% felt children of other races were accepted by other students at school. Few students disagreed with either statement.

*The sum of some survey questions may not add up to 100% because not all respondents answered all questions.

creased understanding and appreciation of what each of us brings to the work environment. These changes become a part of us. We have come to understand that our experiences impact those around us and that we have enormous power to contribute positively to the academic and social development of every student.

LESSONS LEARNED

The Importance of a Team Effort

The successful education of students requires a team effort that extends beyond the classroom. Parents, mentors, and others are a vital part of the educational team, and their role in helping students succeed cannot be overstated. Each student's education must be personalized to meet his or her needs.

Over the years, I have had the opportunity to lead many citizen and staff groups on important topics such as services for dually identified students with disabilities, childhood obesity, underage drinking, substance abuse, anti-bullying, student dropout, and mental health issues which impact youth. As a result, I have come to value diverse points of view. I have learned that the needs of a community are best addressed when the people who are most affected by issues or problems play a part in formulating the solution.

Acceptance of Nonclosure Is Easier Said Than Done

All students deserve to be educated in safe and supportive environments that are built on respectful behaviors, equitable learning opportunities, and culturally responsive teaching. I have been fortunate to have had the opportunity to lead the Arlington Public Schools' cultural competence initiative for seven years. At the end of each training experience I am always moved by the power of individual and collective stories and the reality that there are many things that we do not know. To move forward we must embrace life-long learning.

This Work Requires Reflection and Introspection

Cultural competence work requires courage, patience, passion, willingness to acknowledge what we do not know, and relentless commitment to hold ourselves accountable for results. We are the system.

Elimination of the Achievement Gap Requires a Commitment to the Achievement of All Students

While all districts are held to high stakes testing standards, our educational pedagogy must focus on teaching for meaning. Every student must be exposed to rigorous, challenging, and engaging instructional programs. Students deserve nothing less.

REFERENCES

Ferguson, Ronald F. 2007. *Toward Excellence with Equity: An Emerging Vision for Closing the Achievement Gap.* Cambridge, MA: Harvard Education Press.

Mason, James. 1998. "Developing Cultural Competence for Agencies." *Focal Point* 2: 5–7.

Rutledge, Everard. 2001. "The Struggle for Equality in Healthcare Continues." *Journal of Healthcare Management* 46(5): 313–324.

Singleton, Glenn, and Curtis Linton. 2006. *Courageous Conversations about Race: A Field Guide for Achieving Equity in Schools*. Thousand Oaks, CA: Corwin.

Stinson, Karen. 1991. *Diversity Awareness Profile*. San Francisco: Pfeiffer.

Chapter Nine

Gaining on the Gap: Progress, Themes, and Lessons Learned

Robert G. Smith, Alvin L. Crawley, Cheryl Robinson,
Timothy Cotman Jr., Marty Swaim, and Palma Strand

In this chapter, we pull together the threads presented throughout this book. We begin with an overview of the APS responses and initiatives to achievement gaps, noting measurable accomplishments since 1999 and identifying four stages in this process. We then highlight the central underlying ideas and the characteristics of the cultural competence training that we have developed since 2007. Looking searchingly at all of our chapters together, we discern and describe three overarching themes. Finally, we distill lessons learned overall from the foregoing perspectives.

MAKING PROGRESS

APS has made substantial progress toward the goal of eliminating achievement gaps. The APS efforts, grounded in a broad-based community discussion of crowding, diversity, and educational quality in the mid-1990s, took on a more concrete shape when a school board with newly elected members appointed Rob Smith as superintendent in 1997. Measurable accomplishments have followed:

- Public naming of the problem of achievement gaps and public discussion of the data became the norm.
- Eliminating Achievement Gaps became the APS #2 Strategic Plan Goal in 1999, following the #1 Goal of Rising Achievement for All Students.
- A variety of initiatives have reduced the size of the gaps between Black and Latino and White students on state SOL tests.

- The number of minority students enrolled in advanced classes of all kinds is up by approximately 50%—more in some classes.
- Algebra in the eighth grade is now considered the default for White students. Enrollment and successful completion of Algebra 1 by the end of grade 8 for Black and Latino students has increased by almost 100% and more than 150% respectively. Despite these impressive gains, however, Algebra 1 is not the eighth grade default course for Black and Latino students.
- Other initiatives such as the expansion of TESA training, the preparation of six-year academic plans for all seventh graders, and support for reading instruction have been put in place to address specifically identified needs related to achievement gaps.
- Principals' yearly management plans now address how they will build staff cultural competence to improve student success and reduce achievement gaps.
- The convening of the Superintendent's Advisory Committee on the Elimination of the Achievement Gap and the Council for Cultural Competence as well as a system-wide diversity audit helped create an infrastructure of committed staff and parents and a knowledge basis for moving forward.
- APS has designed and begun training in cultural competence for all administrators and instructional staff. This required training rests on the belief that the success of students of color requires changed staff behaviors in K–12—specifically a consciousness of race, race and schooling, and racial identity development as well as an ability to talk about race and one's own race—that constitute culturally competent teaching and administration.
- Cultural competence training for administrators began in 2007; the training for teachers and staff in 2009–2010. While research evidence suggests that specific teaching behaviors increase the success of students of color, our data about the effects of training in producing these teaching behaviors are early and, as yet, anecdotal.

Looking back on these milestones toward organizational change, we discern four developmental stages. The first stage might be called "preparing the ground": putting the issue of equity for all students on the table and changing the way we talk about achievement gaps. Although this first stage predated 1997, it crystallized in that year when the school board made clear its commitment to addressing that issue by hiring Rob, a superintendent who was willing to state the issue clearly and start working on solutions. The combination of a superintendent seeking to address achievement gaps, a supportive school board, and a community attuned to the issue provided the foundation.

In the second stage, "sowing the seed," the commitment on the part of the board and the superintendent to talk about equity and achievement gaps led to the giant step of talking publicly and honestly about data disaggregated by race and ethnicity. In APS, this step took place five years before No Child Left Behind. APS involved the public in discussions about achievement gaps between Black, Latino, and White students, which were shown clearly by the data.

In this second stage, the question was framed: Can a system be a good system when a significant group of its students is consistently not successful? Over time, a definitive response emerged with increasing clarity: No. Out of the practice of looking at the data came taking responsibility as a school system for what those data showed. The 1999 APS Strategic Goals made concrete this acceptance of school system responsibility.

The third developmental stage began in the midst of these public discussions and actions. This stage, what we might term "tending the crop," was and is programmatic and included

- A six-year plan to support the Strategic Plan Goals adopted by the board.
- Budget initiatives to increase pre-K enrollment in general and for minority students in particular.
- Instructional changes to increase the enrollment of students of color in advanced classes and parental choice regarding student placement in advanced classes.
- Instructional work on teaching for meaning.
- Six-year academic plans for all students, to be prepared with and for rising seventh graders.
- The expansion of TESA training of instructional staff.
- The offering of three different graduate-level classes for staff on diversity and cultural competence—IT MATTERS, Teaching Across Cultures, and SEED—starting in 2000.

As the superintendent and the board began the public conversation about achievement gaps, these program initiatives developed in many places: in the Department of Instruction (with notable leadership by the Office of Minority Achievement); in the Department of Student Services; in the Superintendent's Advisory Committee on Elimination of the Achievement Gap, formed in 1998; and in the system-wide employee Council on Cultural Competence, created in 2003.

By 2005, APS had acknowledged the problem, publicly discussed data on gaps, taken responsibility, and made progress on ensuring equitable opportunity for all students. APS had, in fact, reduced gaps and expanded opportunities for many minority students. But progress had stalled, and longitudinal student data showed the gaps continuing to grow in the key year of third grade.

Logically, we needed to look at some of the more difficult-to-talk-about and complex causes of unacceptably low levels of achievement by minority students. Over time, discussion about the programs that increased opportunities for students of color came back to the basic question of whether we were dealing only with the symptoms of the gaps, and not the cause. How do these gaps start in the first place?

Certainly, some students of color come without the skills and vocabulary they need, especially those for whom English is a second language. But in the APS preschool initiative, minority students leave preschool with the normal range of skills for kindergarten, according to state-required tests. By third grade, their scores, although higher than similarly situated students who did not attend pre-K, are in decline. What happens?

We began to look at the role of race in creating achievement gaps in more and more areas of the institution: curriculum, materials, and staff attitudes about race—their own race and that of their students. *Race in this context refers not to the race of the children on the far side of achievement gaps but to how educators view Black, Latino, and other children of color and how those educator views of people of color produce educator behaviors that ultimately encourage students to flourish—or decline.*

And so the fourth stage—the complex stage of changing hearts, minds, and practices one by one, conversation by conversation, teacher by teacher, administrator by administrator—arrived. This fourth stage might be understood as "cultivating the field"—doing whatever one can to ensure that weeds do not choke, pests do not devour, or disease does not stunt vulnerable plants as they grow.

The important shift in this fourth stage is that the race of the children in achievement gap statistics is no longer the challenge. Rather, it is a barometer of the degree to which the problem of the gap persists. Now the challenge is to help staff begin and continue on the path of self-reflection and assessment about themselves and race.

In general, school systems have not looked at how staff view the race of others and how these perceptions affect their interactions with peers, families, community members, and, most important, children. Schools remain in the mode of conversation about race developed during and after school desegregation: "I do not see race or color or ethnicity; I see a child; I treat all children the same."

The fourth stage requires drawing back the "color blindness" curtain and letting the light of awareness shine on subconscious perceptions and biases as well as the everyday actions in which they are embedded. It is explicit conversations about race that provide the sunlight.

The conventional mode—nonconversation about race—occurs because White teaching staff generally are not aware of the effects of race on their own behavior or on the needs of the children in their classes. White teachers, like most White people, are generally at the stage of racial awareness that leads them to say "I am color-blind." White staff do not need to think about their race because White is the norm.

Racial identity development, however, means that children need to hear adults affirm their identity with positive messages about their race, positive inquiry, materials, and curricula in which children of all races see themselves validated. These all require conversations in which questions about race are discussed, not hushed.

In 2006, the APS conversation moved from programmatic initiatives alone to asking what we could do so that all children were successful. What would have to be different? Building on preexisting but uncoordinated efforts, Rob Smith, the Council on Cultural Competence, and the Office of Minority Achievement took the next step: to develop among our heavily White staff necessary conversations about race and achievement gaps that focus on the race of staff, their perceptions of race and people of color, and sets of stories—Black, White, and Latino. This required training became the Curriculum for Cultural Competence. Required training began in 2007 for all administrators and in 2009–2010 for the teachers and assistants in the first 13 volunteer schools.

CENTRAL IDEAS ON ACHIEVEMENT GAPS AND CULTURAL COMPETENCE TRAINING

A number of central ideas regarding achievement gaps evolved over the years. These essential ideas are outlined here.

Educators Should Not Be Let Off the Hook

The APS goal is to remove race, ethnicity, income, and dominant language as predictors of student achievement. APS views the estimates of the amount of the variance in student learning explained by education factors, such as the 40% reported by Rothstein (2004), as status reports rather than conclusions about the limits of educational influence. They estimate "a current reading . . . as opposed to a ceiling on educational influences."

Rob Smith argues that schools should not evade responsibility by attributing gaps to social factors and that communities—and the nation—should not be held blameless when they do not provide a living wage, housing, health care, and employment. Schools have a fundamental responsibility to use the substantial time each school day that they work with a child to help that child succeed, no matter the responsibilities of other parts of the society.

If we could start over, we would try from the beginning to find partners in the county government: social services, housing, and recreation. Imagine how gains from schools taking responsibility could be compounded by them working hand-in-hand with other community institutions to support children and build resilience in children!

Working Together in This Effort Requires Common Definitions

We use the definition of racism from Beverly Daniel Tatum:

> Racism [is] a "system of advantage based on race." . . . This definition of racism is useful because it allows us to see that racism, like other forms of oppression, is not only a personal ideology based on racial prejudice, but a system involving cultural messages and institutional policies and practices as well as the beliefs and actions of individuals. In the context of

the United States, this system clearly operates to the advantage of Whites and to the disadvantage of people of color. (Tatum 1999, p. 7, quoting Wellman 1977)

This definition shifts the focus from individualized personal prejudice to system results and is expressed in many writings about achievement gaps. It helps us to see the institutional racism of public schools as a system of advantage for White students.

Countering Institutional Racism Requires Challenging Both Policies and Patterns of Behavior

Because APS, like all institutions, sends cultural messages, provides institutional policies, and translates policies into individual actions every day, it is appropriate to talk about how those messages, policies, and actions do or do not support a system of advantage based on race. For example, racial identity development needs to be part of the curriculum. Children develop a racial identity very early. White children, like White adults, are usually not conscious of being White since they do not have to be: they are the norm. Children of color know about color from early consciousness.

Staff in APS need to understand racial identity development, starting with themselves and including their students. Teachers need to learn the skills to be able to talk about race with their students, in the curriculum and as race appears in life, along with the other skills of culturally competent teaching behavior that build success for students of color along with their White peers.

Addressing the Problem as Systemic Is Important

Closing the gap is not the sole responsibility of the Office of Minority Achievement; it is the responsibility of everyone in the school system. Policies arising from APS Strategic Plan Goals contribute to this awareness, as do system-wide structures such as the Council for Cultural Competence and the Superintendent's Advisory Committee on Elimination of the Achievement Gap. Systems are organic and change in reinforcing ways.

This Work Is a Long-Term Proposition;
The Ripples Spread Slowly Over Time

The staff that volunteered to examine their practices in Office of Minority Achievement courses offered between 1998 and 2008 became the core of facilitators who trained to train teachers in 2009. Another core source of facilitators who trained to train teachers in 2009 was the group of 20+ members of the Council for Cultural Competence, which began meeting in 2003. Further, because reexamining experiences and perceptions of race involves deeply rooted and often unconscious views and biases, personal transformation is a long-term journey.

At Any Given Point, New Imperatives and
New Horizons May Appear

This work, which seeks to undo centuries of harm, is likely to outlast our tenure in the system. This is a long-term journey that will require innovation and change as we, and it, progress. Initiatives to address identified problems will take stronger root if the need for change is recognized, the impetus for exploration arises, and the direction forward is set internally.

For example, the need to better measure progress has been identified. The kinds of changes in teacher behavior resulting in better student success described by Tim Cotman and Marty Swaim, in Chapters 6 and 7 respectively, repeated many times over in many different classrooms, are individual interactions that should lead to improved student work. The development of evaluation measures by which to assess such changes—and the cultural competence training from which they arise—must be on the agenda moving forward. At any time, we must be mindful that the current stage of work is not the final stage.

Design of Cultural Competence Training

From these central ideas flows the basic design of the required APS training in cultural competence. We do not delineate the specific design or curriculum of that training in this book, though references to various threads that have been woven together to form the tapestry of that training occur throughout.

The absence of such a description is intentional: What we seek to communicate with this book is how that training emerged from systemic change and how that systemic change came about. The specific configuration of the training, as we have emphasized previously, makes sense for APS in large part because it was developed by and for APS. Because the process of "growing" the training cannot be bypassed, other school systems cannot simply replicate the APS model.

Nonetheless, there are key aspects of the training that we believe are worth emphasizing in terms of overall focus and the general pattern by which the training has evolved. Specifically, we and others who have contributed to this process have

- Begun with self-reflection, identity, and White privilege practices, emphasizing that closing achievement gaps is primarily about changing our own behavior—not that of others.
- Used stories—literary, personal, and guest speakers—to build empathy and understanding so the training operates on the "heart" as well as the "head," a practice well documented to help change behavior in the fields of social work and rehabilitation.
- Allowed time to the extent possible, recognizing that transformations in people's views and actions happen incrementally and often slowly.
- Incorporated practical applications in the form of practice in difficult conversations with others and culturally competent pedagogical strategies so that administrator and teacher "change agents" have concrete tools for change.
- Remembered that one cannot be mad and do this work. The injustice of achievement gaps is maddening, but that anger needs to be channeled as energy into the work of listening, persuading, telling stories, and asking questions.
- Drawn from multiple trainings and sources, but done the hard work of developing the training internally, which has maximized its "fit" with APS as well as buy-in from those responsible for administering it.
- Tried to keep our eyes on the prize of student success.
- Worked hard to frame the reasons for and goals of the training in simple, short, memorable ways—a description that one can offer in the short span of an elevator ride.

- Reflected that all of us have learned something and been transformed by this work. Knowing this helps to maintain the attitude that we are *all* on a journey, that this struggle is for *all* of us. A system-level view tells us not only that we are all part of the problem but that we must also all be part of the solution. Addressing gaps in achievement is everybody's work.
- Responded when training participants complain about "the system": "What does that mean? We *are* the system."
- Started with a small group of volunteers and progressed to a larger segment of APS instructional staff, building on the "early adapters," such as teachers who began in the voluntary training and moved into the APS system-wide training as facilitators for other teachers in training. The process potentially leads to systemic change because it builds practice and commitment at all levels of the system.
- Supported those volunteers. For example, trainees felt that they needed more training in facilitation skills. In response, we have made available to all facilitators intensive training in Results-Based Facilitation.
- Used a "trainer of trainers" model. Volunteer teachers are trained by the first group of volunteer staff who were trained, and the facilitators who do the training are all in-house and primarily teachers themselves.
- Used the local school planning process to get training sites. During the spring period when administrators and staff are talking about next year's training needs, we have offered the cultural competence training as a choice. So although once chosen the training is mandatory within the school, the school chooses the training in its planning process.

We have not eliminated achievement gaps. We have more Black, Latino, and other minority students in advanced classes, but not in proportion to their numbers in our population. Our 2009 figures still show a decline in the scores of students of color after third grade. About 40% of our Black students read below grade level in sixth grade. For those students whom we have not reached—and for the rest of us—this is a tragedy. The need for change is urgent.

When we write that this is a journey, we are not using a metaphor. We believe we see the road ahead, and it is the work of changing behavior all through the system so that students who come to it who do not look like most of the staff find school a place where they can and will be successful.

THEMES

As we look over our distinct accounts of this concerted, system-wide effort to eliminate achievement gaps in the Arlington Public Schools, we identify three recurring themes. The first theme relates to the *what*: the need to put race as an issue squarely on the table. The second concerns the *why*: the reasons that justify devoting the resources of a school system and of a community to this effort. The third focuses on the *when*—specifically on the continuation of the past and current initiatives we have described here into the future.

In our discussions of the first theme, one of us floated the phrase "outing race" to describe the phenomenon of making people's experiences with, awareness of, and assumptions about race and people of various races overt and explicit. The experiences, awareness, and assumptions are there, but too often they are covert and implicit. We agreed that outing race in various contexts and ways is a common thread for all of us.

- For Rob Smith, outing race meant publicly articulating a strategic plan and goal related to achievement gaps, collecting and reporting data presenting those gaps on a systemic basis, budgeting resources for initiatives aimed at reducing them, ensuring that goals relating to eliminating achievement gaps are in each principal's annual work plan, and creating institutional mechanisms such as the Superintendent's Advisory Committee on the Elimination of the Achievement Gap and the Council for Cultural Competence that had explicit charges to examine achievement gaps in APS.
- For Alvin Crawley, outing race has meant convening and facilitating the Council for Cultural Competence, serving as the APS point person for the diversity audit the council recommended, carefully examining statistics and practices related to special education and to administering discipline, and working with Cheryl Robinson and others to develop and systematize the Cultural Competence Curriculum.
- For Cheryl Robinson, outing race has meant developing and providing cultural competence professional development for instructional personnel, serving as a resource for changes in practice related to better instruction of minority students, serving as the staff liaison to the Superintendent's Advisory Committee on the Elimination of the Achieve-

ment Gap, and working to strengthen the "voice" of APS students and parents of color.

• For Marty Swaim, Tim Cotman, and Palma Strand, outing race has meant contributing to the development of the cultural competence training, participating as members of the Superintendent's Advisory Committee on the Elimination of the Achievement Gap, and taking cultural competence to a broader audience as facilitators of groups and in our own interactions with students, parents, and teachers.

For all of us, the task has been to patiently but insistently continue to raise the issue. Once the issue is raised, we seek to overcome the fears associated with the conversation—the fears Whites have of being accused of being racist and the fears people of color have of being hurt. In doing this, we try to create a safe but uncomfortable space in which people can grow and change. We try, in this regard, to call out the best in people—their ability to reach out, to understand, to experience shared humanity across social difference. In this work, each of us takes seriously and personally the ideas "I am the system" and as such "I am part of the solution as well as part of the problem."

The second theme is the conviction that this work is necessary. As we see it, there are at least four distinct rationales that support this conclusion. The first two track philosophical approaches of long standing; the latter two take less familiar paths but ultimately reach the same destination.

The first is grounded in the moral imperative of valuing all human beings. In this view, "seeing" and "respecting" people leads inevitably to slicing through the social construct of race and honoring the essential humanity of each person, of each child. Achievement gaps are tangible proof that we are not living up to this ideal.

The second path leads to the same result via the consequentialist view that we are hurting everyone by allowing an entire group of young people to fall by the wayside. All of the contributions they might make—civic, economic, political, intellectual, artistic, athletic—are diminished when we accept their lesser status. These lost benefits then must be added to the costs that accrue when we fail to educate citizens: underemployment, unemployment, social services, and prison.

A third path acknowledges the importance of groups in our public life. We are not isolated individuals but situated members of groups with salient political and psychological identities. Racial and ethnic identities are a fact of life in our society. The task is not to deny their existence but to acknowledge and to the extent possible equalize existing power differentials (Young 1990). Achievement gaps remind us that power differentials persist.

Finally, from a developmental perspective, schools are a "critical place where we can educate White youth as racial beings" (Denevi 2004). White identity development has been shown to be associated with fewer racist beliefs in college students (Carter 1990) and may counter less intentional White socialization leading to White anxiety regarding interactions with people of color (Marshall 2002). Educators, then, are doing White students specifically, and our future society overall, a major disservice if we do not lay the groundwork for healthy interracial interactions in today's multiracial, multiethnic world.

The third and final theme is the sustainability of the efforts we describe in this book. The life of a system exceeds that of the time any given individual is in it. Transforming the character of a system thus means more than changing the individuals who comprise it at any given point in time.

APS has been accepting lower quality education for children of color for a long time. We see achievement gaps as simply the current manifestation of this deep-seated feature of the system. The imperative of sustainability with respect to the move to eliminate achievement gaps recognizes that systemic change must outlast all of us.

Three efforts are in process to enhance the sustainability of the achievement gap initiative we have described here. The first is the system-wide training itself. A common feature of school systems—of any bureaucracy in which the personnel remain constant while leadership at the top changes—is the ability of the long-term members of the system to outlast desired changes the temporary people put in place.

In contrast, the cultural competence training is designed not simply to change what people within the system are doing in response to *this* school board and *this* superintendent but to change how *they* perceive themselves, their work, and the children they teach. To the extent that APS staff has converted to the view of being part of the solution as well as part of the problem, these efforts will be self-sustaining after a given administration is gone.

Not that administration is unimportant. Far from it: Continuity at the top, at the policy-making level, is essential. Maintaining such continuity is the second effort.

In that regard, we view it as highly promising that the commitment to eliminate achievement gaps remains strong at the time of this writing even though only one member, Libby Garvey, of the original five school board members who hired Rob to be superintendent remains. Rob has, moreover, retired, and a new superintendent, Patrick Murphy, has taken his place. It is a sign of the new superintendent's and the new school board members' investment in this work that they have themselves undertaken training in cultural competence (see Afterword).

Last but far from least, a culture of assessment has been taking hold over the past 10 years. This culture, though it may have been prompted by equity issues, extends beyond them. It is, in fact, a new way for a school system to undertake its work.

Traditionally, school systems have either measured inputs (often in the form of per-pupil spending) rather than outputs (how well its students and graduates were faring) or not viewed measured outputs as indicators of what changes in inputs should be considered. In contrast, much of the work described here was based on data collected about outputs (student results of varying sorts). These data were then evaluated and, where deemed unacceptable, used as the basis for developing proposed changes from business as usual: trying new instructional techniques and professional development.

This is the essence of the individual processes Marty Swaim describes in her chapter, Chapter 7. It is, moreover, the mindset that led to the cultural competence training: Obvious initiatives were reducing but not eliminating the gaps, which called for a more far-reaching initiative.

An assessment culture is based on this feedback loop: data, evaluation, response. And it is this loop, assimilated into the system's way of doing business that becomes the mechanism for system evolution and adaptation. Information provides the basis for change—not in the sense of doing more of the same but in the sense of addressing the problem by changing the ways in which the organization treats the problem, questioning norms, values, and protocols, and changing hearts, minds, and practice (Argyris and Schon 1974).

We are aware, in this regard, of the importance of measuring the cultural competence training itself. Developing measures of the training will clarify both its precise contribution and how it works to effect change overall. This new understanding will lay the foundation for the next "tweak" of the system in a continuing process of improvement.

Overall, then, the themes we see as recurring throughout all of our accounts in this decade-long effort to eliminate achievement gaps in APS are three:

- The first is *the need to "out" race*. Race must be on the table—in data, in policy discussions, in employee forums, in professional development, in classrooms, in hallway and faculty lounge conversations. Conversations about race lay the necessary groundwork for stripping it of its talismanic, predictive power.
- The second is *the conviction that the work is necessary*. Though this conviction may rest on different philosophical or psychological views, it renders urgency to the work. This is not "feel good," optional work. This is "must-do" work: We must do it if we are to do our jobs properly.
- The third is a constant awareness that *sustainability must be built into every change* if what we do is to take root. We are ambitious, and we see the need for lasting, systemic change. Our goal is not only to make a change for the kids who are in APS this year and next year but the kids who come ten, twenty, and more years down the road.

LESSONS LEARNED

Each of us individually has offered lessons learned that are specific to our own role and experiences as part of the preceding chapters. We also include here lessons learned highlights (Table 9.1), which we believe provide an impressionistic portrait of *systemic* lessons learned through the process we have described. These lessons learned, we believe, provide touchstones for people in other public school systems that have joined or seek to join us on this journey.

The purpose of this book is to tell the story of systemic change by telling the individual stories of people with various roles in APS and its efforts to eliminate achievement gaps. The sections of this chapter capture the essential progress APS as a whole has made in "gaining on the gap" in several different ways:

- We have described the chronological stages of the APS response to the problem.

Table 9.1.   Selected Lessons Learned by Perspective of Position

Superintendent's Perspective	Senior Staff Member's Perspective	Parent's Perspective	Facilitator's Perspective	We All Learned
Apply Principles Rather Than Replicate Procedures. We will experience greater success if we capture the principles of efforts believed to be effective elsewhere and then adapt the procedures to local conditions, our needs and our strengths.	*Everyone's Responsibility.* Closing the gap is not the responsibility of just one of-fice; it is the responsibility of everyone in the system.	*Invite Parents to Share Their Views.* Parents and other adults should be invited to contribute what they can rather than be blamed for what they can't or don't.	*Continue to Strengthen Facilitation Skills.* It is not enough to have a passion for the work, you need to have the skills necessary to facilitate. Use teachers to train teachers, which provides credibility and skills.	*Confront Race.* Achievement gaps will remain large and progress will stall unless we confront directly the issue of race in ways that allow all of us to understand the impact of our own race on the problem
Good Intentions Are Insuf-ficient. Good intentions must be married to knowledge of the principles that must be implemented, provision of the necessary resources, and persistence in the face of adversity and failure.	*Multiple Voices.* It is impor-tant to have input from a va-riety of stakeholders in order to ensure that we incorporate a wide range of perspectives. Continue to ask the question, "Who is not present at the table?"	*Create a Continuing Advisory Body Including Parents and Community Members* whose job is to push the issue and provide accountability.	*Stories, Stories, Stories.* Stories are the best way to bridge social fault lines of race, ethnicity, religion, so-cioeconomics, institutional role, and religion. Stories give people access to each other's humanity.	*Recruit Allies.* While schools can make progress and should be held responsible for doing so, this problem is too big for schools to handle alone. New forms of cooperation need to be invented or pursued.
Build on Strengths. We make progress when we build on strengths and allow one success to inform the next, rather than attack real or imagined deficits, or attack people rather than problems.	*We Are the system.* Challenging institutional racism requires challenging both policies and patterns of behavior.	*Provide Multiple Forums for People* in different roles to talk to each other about achievement gaps, institu-tional racism, and cultural competence.	*Give People Concrete Tools* for changing their behavior or help them develop their own. Difficult conversations, organizing techniques, and instructional practices are examples.	*Build Capacity.* It is important to do this work on different fronts. If school personnel, community members, parents, and students are having the same conversations, there is greater momentum to moving forward.

(continued)

Table 9.1. Selected Lessons Learned by Perspective of Position (continued)

Superintendent's Perspective	Senior Staff Member's Perspective	Parent's Perspective	Facilitator's Perspective	We All Learned
Public Reporting and Accountability are the starting points for system progress.	*The Problem Isn't with the Students; It Is With The School System.* This means that our focus must be on changing how the system and people in the system operate.	*Institutional Racism* is the everyday actions of individuals within the school system.	*Start With Volunteers* to initiate the conversation about race and the achievement gap. These volunteers provide a high level of thoughtfulness and knowledge of the issues in the training because of their experiences talking about race and achievement over time.	*This Work Is Necessary.* Educators are doing our future society a disservice if we do not lay the groundwork for healthy interracial interactions in today's—and tomorrow's—multicultural world.
	There Is a Strong Connection Between "Diversity" Issues for School System Staff as Employees and "diversity" issues for school system staff as they interact with students.		*White People Need to Talk to Other White People* about race, racial identity development, and the connection between race and the achievement gap.	*Sustainability Is the Ultimate Goal.* Only transforming the system itself will result in changes that benefit children both now and into the future.

- We have identified the assumptions that underlie the APS initiatives.
- We have summarized essential characteristics of the cultural competence training APS developed when earlier initiatives stalled.
- We have surfaced recurrent themes that weave through the APS work in this area over the past decade.
- We have presented the lessons learned from varying perspectives of people within the system.

We hope that one or more of these stories will resonate, will inspire others to begin or continue or deepen this work, and will provide new and useful perspectives on how it can be undertaken.

REFERENCES

Argyris, Chris, and Donald Schon. 1974. *Theory in Practice: Increasing Professional Effectiveness*. San Francisco: Jossey-Bass.

Carter, Robert. 1990. "The Relationship between Racism and Racial Identity among White Americans: An Exploratory Investigation." *Journal of Counseling and Development* 69: 46–50.

Denevi, Elizabeth. 2004. "White on White: Exploring White Racial Identity, Privilege, and Racism." *Independent School Magazine*, Summer 2004. Retrieved November 2010 from http://www.nais.org/ismagazinearticlePrint.cfm?print=Y&ItemNumber=147150

Marshall, Patricia L. 2002. "Racial Identity and Challenges of Educating White Youths for Cultural Diversity." *Multicultural Perspectives* 4(3): 9–14.

Rothstein, Richard. 2004. *Class and Schools: Using Social, Economic and Educational Reform to Close the Black-White Achievement Gap*. Washington, DC: Economic Policy Institute.

Tatum, Beverly Daniel. 1999. *Why Are All the Black Kids Sitting Together in the Cafeteria? And Other Conversations about Race: A Psychologist Explains the Development of Racial Identity*. New York: Basic Books.

Wellman, David. 1977. *Portraits of White Racism*. Cambridge: Cambridge University Press.

Young, Iris Marion. 1990. *Justice and the Politics of Difference*. Princeton, NJ: Princeton University Press.

Afterword

Patrick K. Murphy

In 2009, I had the good fortune of joining the Arlington Public Schools as the new superintendent as the district celebrated the retirement of Robert Smith. I was aware of the many achievements of the Arlington community and school division, and was drawn to the district because of its commitment to provide all students with the opportunity to succeed in all areas of their lives.

One of the key priorities of the district was the work to eliminate the achievement gap between White, Black, and Latino students. Not surprisingly, this topic elicits a great deal of passion and emotion from all stakeholders given the significant impact low student achievement has on access to rigorous courses, graduation rates, college acceptance rates and, ultimately, employment and becoming productive citizens in our community. Most importantly, it becomes a reflection of our ability to prepare all of our students to be capable adults with the skills to live and work successfully in our very competitive global society.

Gaining on the Gap: Changing Hearts, Minds, and Practice takes us on the first leg of Arlington Public Schools' journey to confront and address, like school districts across the nation, that there are serious disparities in student performance by race on a number of educational measures.

The authors suggest that this is a journey of continuous improvement, and they emphasize the need for collective responsibility for change. How does it happen? We know that the key ingredients include sustained professional development; analysis and use of various student data disaggregated; initiatives to build strong relationships with students and families; and a commitment to organizational cultural competence.

Cultural competence includes honest conversations about racial identity and privilege; the role of race in learning; educator behaviors that support or undermine the academic, social, and emotional growth of students of color; and development of clear indicators and effective strategies that show we are experiencing success in eliminating racial gaps in achievement. Arlington Public Schools began this initiative in 2008 with administrators.

Last year, the district's effort expanded to include facilitated conversations with school staff members, and I joined the school board members for their monthly discussions. The involvement of the school board along with our administrators and staff in this important initiative is a testament to the district leadership's commitment at all levels to this important work.

This year, Arlington is embarking on the development of a new six-year strategic plan. What remains key and central to our mission is the commitment to raise achievement for all students and the elimination of race as a predictor of student success.

By building on the good work that has been done, Arlington is well positioned to bring about the reforms necessary to meet the educational needs of all its students. We can fulfill this aspiration with careful planning, thorough analysis of data, and a laser-like focus on meeting our goals—being constantly aware that what gets measured gets done. While we need to be strategic in our thinking and planning, we must continue to align and integrate our analyses, resources, and actions. Our time is measured in years, not decades, in order to make a difference in the life of every child.

Change happens when we are willing to hold ourselves accountable for results and learn from mistakes. There is still much work to be done, and we are committed to do what we have to do to succeed. We must build on the knowledge and learning that have brought us to this point, all the while looking on the horizon to see the next steps of our journey. When we close the achievement gap we will know that we have arrived. Our children are too important to do anything less.

Index

About the Authors

Robert G. Smith, B.A., M.A., Ph.D., is currently an associate professor in the George Mason University's College of Education and Human Development's Education Leadership program. Smith retired from K–12 public education in July 2009 after 44 years as a K–12 public school educator, working as a teacher, building administrator, central office administrator, and superintendent. In his last position he served 12 years as the superintendent of the Arlington Public Schools, preceded by 16 years in the Spring Independent School District in Houston, Texas, and 16 years in the Frederick County, Maryland, Public Schools.

Alvin L. Crawley, B.S., M.S., Ed.D., is assistant superintendent for student services in the Arlington Public Schools. He also co-chairs the school system's Council for Cultural Competence, which focuses its work on systemic changes to address achievement gaps. He became interested in pursuing research related to the relationship between cultural competence and student achievement after participating in several diversity training workshops, including Seeking Educational Equity and Diversity (SEED). Crawley has also worked as a teacher, speech-language pathologist, special education administrator, and adjunct professor.

Cheryl Robinson, B.A., M.Ed., is the supervisor for the Office of Minority Achievement for the Arlington Public Schools. In this capacity, Robinson coordinates professional development opportunities for school employees focusing on the ways that schools can improve the delivery of services to students and families of diverse backgrounds. She also coordinates enrichment opportunities for students and parents. Robinson has been happily married for 24 years and is the mother of three daughters.

Timothy Cotman Jr., B.A., M.Ed., is a minority achievement coordinator with the Arlington Public Schools, a position he has held since 1996. His role within the school system presents him with the opportunity to work with students, families, and staff on initiatives to eliminate achievement gaps. He continues to strengthen his skills as a facilitator and search for ways to create more equitable learning environments.

Marty Swaim, B.A., M.A., pulls together multiple threads from a long career in education in her current work as a cultural competence trainer. She was a member of the first elected Board of Education in Washington, DC, and later a secondary social studies teacher in the Arlington Public Schools. In the latter role, Swaim served three terms as the elected president of the Arlington Education Association. She has also been a teacher consultant to the Northern Virginia Writing Project and an instructor at George Mason University.

Palma Strand, B.S., J.D., LL.M., is an associate professor at Creighton Law School in Omaha, Nebeaska. When her oldest child headed to kindergarten in the Arlington Public Schools in 1992, Strand sought a diverse school in which all kids were doing well. This quest led to work as a community member on achievement gaps and then to cultural competence training, which provided language and skills for grappling with her experiences as a white parent with biracial children. She continues to pursue issues of equity—in education and more broadly in the legal field.